西安交通大学"十四五"规划教材
西安交通大学少年班规划教材·英语

BRIDGE TO COLLEGE

交流与表达（2）

COMMUNICATION FOR ACADEMIC STUDY

牛莉 ◎ 总主编
龚颖 成旻 ◎ 本册主编
成旻 龚颖 郭金华 刘晏辰 牛莉 ◎ 编者

西安交通大学出版社
XI'AN JIAOTONG UNIVERSITY PRESS

国家一级出版社
全国百佳图书出版单位

图书在版编目(CIP)数据

　　交流与表达. 2:英文 / 牛莉总主编；龚颖，成旻本册主编. —西安：西安交通大学出版社，2021.1
　　ISBN 978-7-5693-2000-8

　　Ⅰ.①交… Ⅱ.①牛… ②龚… ③成… Ⅲ.①英语-口语-高等学校-教材 Ⅳ.①H319.9

　　中国版本图书馆 CIP 数据核字(2020)第 263664 号

书　　名	交流与表达(2)
总　主　编	牛　莉
本册主编	龚　颖　成　旻
责任编辑	李　蕊
出版发行	西安交通大学出版社 (西安市兴庆南路 1 号　邮政编码 710048)
网　　址	http://www.xjtupress.com
电　　话	(029)82668357　82667874(发行中心) (029)82668315(总编办)
传　　真	(029)82668280
印　　刷	广东虎彩云印刷有限公司
开　　本	710mm×1000mm　1/16　　印张　10.25　　字数　253 千字
版次印次	2021 年 1 月第 1 版　2021 年 1 月第 1 次印刷
书　　号	ISBN 978-7-5693-2000-8
定　　价	42.00 元

如发现印装质量问题,请与本社发行中心联系。
订购热线:(029)82665248　(029)82665249
投稿热线:(029)82668531　(029)82665371
读者信箱:xjtu_rw@163.com

版权所有　侵权必究

总序 Foreword

　　1985年对西安交通大学来说是一个值得铭记的年份。这一年,教育部正式批准学校开办少年班,学校积极响应邓小平同志的指示:"在人才的问题上,要特别强调一下,必须打破常规去发现、选拔和培养杰出的人才。"转眼间,少年班已走过了三十五年的办学历程,在破解"如何发现智力超常少年并因材施教"这一极具挑战性的难题上,西安交通大学先后有五位校长,他们艰难探索,矢志不渝,构建了一套适合中国国情且自主创新的少年班人才选拔和培养体系,培养了一批又一批少年英才。目前,少年班从初中应届毕业生中选拔招生,实行"预科—本科—硕士"八年制贯通培养模式,其中,预科一年级在指定的四所优秀预科中学学习,预科二年级在大学学习,各为期一年。

　　基础教育与高等教育的有机衔接一直是少年班探索和研究的重点,而教材作为知识衔接的重要载体,成为影响少年班教育质量的关键因素。为此,钱学森学院于2010年10月成立少年班教材编写小组,正式启动教材编写研究工作。全国首套少年班系列教材出版于2014年12月。来自大学及高中的近60名专家和一线教师参与其中,谨遵"因材施教,发掘潜能,注重创新,超常教育,培养英才"的指导思想,通过多次研讨、仔细斟酌、反复修订和严格审核,耗时四年有余,最终编写并出版了全国首套将"预科—本科"有机衔接的教材。这套教材包含六门课程,共22册,总计2550学时,828万字。这套教材自出版至今,使用效果良好。

　　2018年,经过大量调研,钱学森学院制定了新版少年班培养方案,在新版培养方案的基础上规划修订数学、物理、化学、英语等课程的教材,并于2020年启动少年班"十四五"规划教材的编写出版工作。此版教材将力求实现"预科—本科"课程的无缝衔接,从知识体系、内容结构、案例设计、习题配套等方面对教材内涵和风格进行重新编撰和优化,同时注重拔尖学生的发展需求,体现新版少年班培养方案中"以兴趣为导向"的教育教学改革思想。

　　愿此版教材可让更多关注少年班的有识之士受益。同时,我们也希望借此机会,号召大家集思广益,群策群力,共同为推动少年英才培养进程做出努力。

　　是为序。

杨　森

2020年8月10日

前言 Preface

从2012年开始接手少年班的教学工作,我们的教学团队一直在探索适合少年班的英语教学模式,包括课程设置、教学内容、教学方法与手段、评价方式及教材等。2018年我校钱学森学院重新制定了少年班培养方案,我们团队也借此机会对我们的教学模式重新进行了梳理,决定开设两门英语课程:"阅读与写作(Reading and Writing for Academic Study)"和"交流与表达(Communication for Academic Study)"。因此,为这两门课程而编写的两套同名教材应运而生。同时,基于少年班英语课程培养方案的总目标,即"帮助学生完成从通用英语(English for General Purpose, EGP)到学业英语(English for Academic Study, EAS)的过渡,为学生进入大学学习做好语言能力的准备",我们又将这两套教材的编写内容进行了有机结合,构成了"通往大学"系列(*Bridge to College*)。

本系列教材有三个特色:

一、教材编写突出体现"以学习为中心"和"以成果为导向"的教学理念,如下图所示:

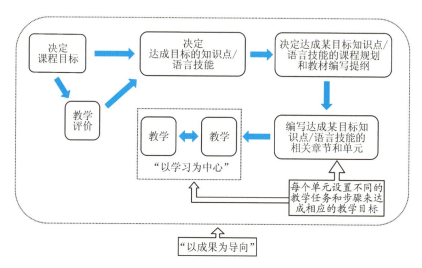

二、教材章节编排侧重构建英语语言知识和技能体系。与一般英语教材中以话题为章节(theme-based)的编写原则不同,本教材采用以功能为章节(function-based,即突出对语言知识点和技能的培养)的编写原则。因为,以话题为章节的编写理念侧重扩充相关话题的词汇量或表达,忽视了语言知识点或

语言技能之间的相关性,缺乏系统性,会导致学生在学习之后只能想起某些课文的内容;而本教材以功能为章节进行编写,其目的在于帮助学生获得相关知识点或技能,同时也帮助学生构建出完整的英语语言知识和技能体系。

三、教材内容融入教学设计。本教材中的各个章节,不仅是学生应掌握的相关知识点,同时也是教师在教学中的具体目标。本教材的章节编排突破了传统英语教材"课文+练习"的模式,变为"通过设置不同的教学任务和步骤来达成相应的教学目标"的模式。这样的编写模式,既包含了学生学习的过程,也体现了教师教学的过程,实现了"以学习为中心",即"教师为主导,学生为主体"的教学理念。

基于上述编写特点,本系列教材也适用于高中生和本科生自主学习。

最后,特别感谢各位编写老师牺牲难得的假期投入教材编写工作!特别感谢西安交通大学附属中学的刘晏辰老师对预科一年级教材初稿的试用和及时的意见反馈!特别感谢少年班 2017 级、2018 级的同学们对教材讲义试用和新教学模式探索的积极配合和肯定!特别感谢西安交通大学钱学森学院和外国语学院给予我们团队的各种支持!特别感谢我们教学团队(包括各中学和大学的所有老师)的辛勤付出!

牛 莉

2020 年暑假

SECTION 1   Speaking Appropriately

Module 1   Making Small Talk /003

Module 2   Speaking Formally or Informally /008

Module 3   Speaking Directly or Indirectly /015

Module 4   Making Direct or Indirect Suggestions /021

Module 5   Making a Polite Request /027

Module 6   Making a Serious and Formal Invitation /035

Module 7   Accepting or Declining an Invitation /040

Module 8   Making Apologies /045

SECTION 2   Communicating in Daily Life

Module 9   Finding the Right Words to Express Yourself /055

Module 10   Airport or Railway Station /060

Module 11   Restaurants /071

Module 12   Hotel /078

Module 13   Travel /086

Module 14   Shopping /094

Module 15   Visiting a Doctor /103

Module 16   Asking and Giving Directions /109

SECTION 3 Making One-Minute Presentations

Module 17 Making a Good One-Minute Presentation /117

Module 18 Expanding Ideas in Presentation: Description /122

Module 19 Expanding Ideas in Presentation: Giving Definition /128

Module 20 Expanding Ideas in Presentation: Classification /132

Module 21 Expanding Ideas in Presentation: Process /136

Module 22 Expanding Ideas in Presentation: Comparison and Contrast /140

Module 23 Expanding Ideas in Presentation: Cause and Effect /144

Module 24 Expanding Ideas in Presentation: Problem-Solution /148

Module 25 Expanding Ideas in Presentation: Argumentation /152

SECTION 1

Speaking Appropriately

Module 1 Making Small Talk

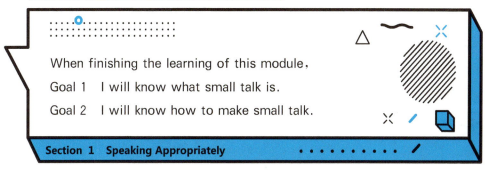

When finishing the learning of this module,
Goal 1   I will know what small talk is.
Goal 2   I will know how to make small talk.

Section 1   Speaking Appropriately

TASK

Making Small Talk

Warming up

Work in pairs and answer the questions.

1. If you meet a stranger, are you the person who breaks the ice? Why or why not?
2. What topics have you used to make a conversation with a stranger?

BRIDGE to COLLEGE
交流与表达 2 COMMUNICATION FOR ACADEMIC STUDY (2)

 **ACTIVITY 2**

Understanding small talk

Step 1

Watch the conversation and fill in the blanks.

Part Ⅰ

Man: _____?

Woman: Well, I've seen it better, but this is OK.

Man: _____?

Woman: Yes, I do. I go as often as I can.

Man: Me, too. By the way, my name's Alan Ross.

Woman: How do you do. I'm Dianne Cooper.

Part Ⅱ

Woman: _____, Mr. Ross?

Man: No, I don't. _____ Los Angeles.

Woman: Have you lived in Los Angeles long?

Man: No, only for the last two years. Before that, I lived in Chicago.

Woman: _____.

Man: It's a great place.

Part Ⅲ

Man: _____?

Woman: Oh, different things, _____. How about you?

Man: On weekends _____. I need the exercise.

Woman: I don't enjoy _____. I'm not really _____.

Module 1 Making Small Talk

Watch the conversation again to see how the speakers *start* and *continue* their conversation.

Work in pairs and fill in the blanks with the topics in the conversation.

A Small Talk

| Opening | Greeting | The play they were watching | Introduction |

| Continuing | | | |

| Ending | Saying goodbye |

Role play the conversation with a partner.

BRIDGE TO COLLEGE
交流与表达 2 COMMUNICATION FOR ACADEMIC STUDY (2)

Step 5

Watch a video clip about a blind date. <u>Underline</u> the *improper topics* you think in this small talk.

Penny: So are the rest of the guys meeting us here?

Leonard: Oh, yeah... no.

Leonard: It turns out that Raj and Howard had to work, and Sheldon had a colonoscopy and he hasn't quite bounced back yet.

Penny: Oh, my uncle just had a colonoscopy.

Leonard: You're kidding. Then that's something we have in common.

Penny: How?

Leonard: We both have people in our lives who want to nip intestinal polyps in the bud.

Penny: So what's new in the world of physics?

Leonard: Nothing.

Penny: Really? Nothing?

Leonard: Well, with the exception of string theory, not much has happened since the 1930s. And you can't prove string theory. At best you can say, "hey, look, my idea has an internal logical consistency."

Penny: Ah. Well, I'm sure things will pick up.

Leonard: What's new at the Cheesecake Factory?

Penny: Oh, uh, not much. We do have a chocolate key lime that's moving pretty well.

Leonard: Good. Good. What about your, hallway friend?

Penny: Doug? Oh, yeah, I don't know. I mean, you know, he's nice and funny, but...

Waitress: Can I get you started with some drinks?

Module 1 Making Small Talk

Leonard: No! You were saying? But…

Penny: I'd like a drink.

Leonard: Just say the "but" thing about Doug and then I'll get her back.

Penny: Okay, well, I don't know, it's just me. I'm still getting over this breakup with Kurt.

Making small talk

Work in pairs and make small talk with the situations given below.

Situation 1: the first time you met your new English teacher in the classroom

Situation 2: the first time of a day you met someone you know on the campus

Situation 3: the first time you met a friend of one of your friends in your dorm

Listen to "Small Talk" and answer the following questions:

1. According to the listening material, what is small talk?
2. Whom will we make small talk with?
3. What are the tips for making small talk?

Module 2 Speaking Formally or Informally

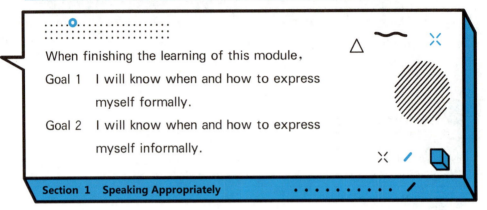

When finishing the learning of this module,

Goal 1   I will know when and how to express myself formally.

Goal 2   I will know when and how to express myself informally.

Section 1   Speaking Appropriately

TASK ONE
Speaking Formally or Informally

Warming up

Read the expressions and discuss with your partner if there is any difference between the ways of expressing in column A and B.

Module 2 Speaking Formally or Informally

A	B
Hey, hi.	Hello, doctor/Mr. Smith.
How ya doin'? —I'm doin' good.	How are you? —I'm fine. Thank you.
Ann, this is Jim. He's in my class. —Hi Jim. Nice to meet you.	Dr. White, I'd like to introduce you to Rachel. —It's a pleasure to meet you. —Pleased to meet you.
Nice meeting you. —You too.	It was nice meeting you. —It was nice meeting you, too.
I'm off. —OK, bye.	Have a good day. —Thank you. You too.
I gotta go. —See ya. —Bye.	Good night / Goodbye. —Good night / Goodbye.
Please don't smoke.	Please refrain from smoking.
Y'wanna go to the dance tonight?	Do you want to go to the dance tonight?
That sucks.	That's too bad.

Results of your discussion

BRIDGE TO COLLEGE
交流与表达 2 COMMUNICATION FOR ACADEMIC STUDY (2)

 ACTIVITY 2 ▶

Understanding formality and informality

Listen to the passage three times, and fill in the blanks.

You probably have noticed that people express similar ideas in different ways depending on the (1) _____ they are in. This is very natural. (2) _____. English is no (3) _____. The difference in these two levels is the situation in which you use a (4) _____ level. Formal language is the kind of language you find in textbooks, (5) _____ books and in business letters. You would also use formal English in (6) _____ that you write in school. Informal language is used in conversation with (7) _____, family members and friends, and when we write (8) _____ or letters to close friends. Formal language is different from informal language in several ways. First, (9) _____. What we may find interesting is that it usually takes more words to be polite. For example, I might say to a friend or a family member "Close the door, please", (10) _____. Another difference between formal and informal language is some of the vocabulary. (11) _____. Let's say that I really like soccer. If I am talking to my friend, I might say "I am just crazy about soccer", but if I were talking to my boss, I would probably say "I really enjoy soccer".

Module 2　Speaking Formally or Informally

Step 2

Listen to the passage again to write down the information related to the formal and informal expressions.

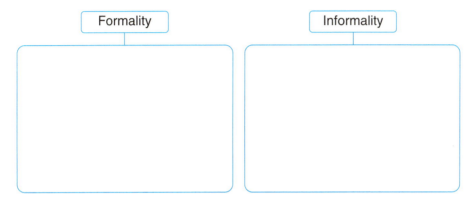

Step 3

Work in pairs and take a short quiz.

1. You are meeting your host parents in America for the first time. What is the best way to greet them?
   A. Hey, what's up?
   B. It is a pleasure to meet you.
   C. Hello, nice to meet you.

2. You are meeting your best friend from Australia for dinner. You haven't seen each other for a while. What is the best way to greet them?
   A. Long time no see. What's up?
   B. I haven't seen you for such a long time. It's a pleasure to see you again.
   C. Hi.

3. **Boss**: Hey Carlos, can ya (you) help me for a sec?
   Carlos: Yes, what do you need?
   Boss: Can ya fax this to ABC company ASAP.
   What should Carlos say next?
   A. Yes sir. I'll be happy to do that right away for you.
   B. Sure, no prob.
   C. My pleasure. I'd love to fax that report.

TASK TWO

Understanding Differences between Formality and Informality

Understanding language features of formality and informality

Step 1

Watch a video clip from the film *Bridget Jones: The Edge of Reason*.

Module 2 Speaking Formally or Informally

Step 2

Read the transcripts of the video clip you've watched. Underline the formal expressions and highlight the informal ones.

> **Bridget:** I love you. I always have and I always will. Oh, I don't love you, and I never have, and… I never will. Sorry.
>
> …
>
> **Darcy:** Come in. Hello, Bridget.
>
> **Bridget:** Hello, Mark. Er… I'm sorry, I'm disturbing you.
>
> …
>
> **Bridget:** Well, I just wanted to tell Mr. Darcy here that I heard what magnificent work he actually did releasing me from prison.
>
> **Bridget:** And I also wanted to say, … that I love him. Always have. Always will. And that I'm… you know… available for dates… if he should feel so inclined.

Step 3

Watch the video clip again. Discuss with your partner on the questions: On what occasion did BJ change her language style? Why?

Results of your discussion

BRIDGE TO COLLEGE
交流与表达 ❷ COMMUNICATION FOR ACADEMIC STUDY (2)

Step 4

Discuss with your partner and fill in the blanks.

Elements	Formal Expression	Informal Expression
Length of Sentence		
Structure of Sentence		
Language		
Ways of Addressing		

ASSIGNMENTS

Expressing yourself formally and informally: Work in pairs or groups and make a conversation with the situations

Situation 1 Imagine you are on a plane flying to New York. You are sitting next to someone your age. First, think of three or four topics of conversation that would be appropriate to discuss with this person. Then, make a conversation with your partners in proper language style.

Situation 2 Imagine you are going to have a job interview for a journalist position. Make a conversation with your partners in proper language.

Module 3　Speaking Directly or Indirectly

Module 3　Speaking Directly or Indirectly

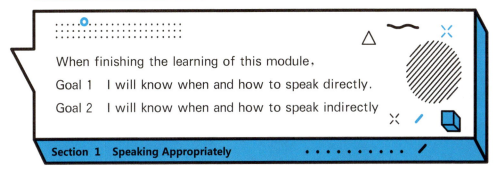

When finishing the learning of this module,

Goal 1　I will know when and how to speak directly.

Goal 2　I will know when and how to speak indirectly

Section 1　Speaking Appropriately

TASK ONE
Speaking Directly or Indirectly

Warming up

Discuss with your partner on the situations below.

Situation 1
I know someone is being direct with me when they _____

Situation 2
If I want to say something that may hurt someone's feelings, I _____

交流与表达 **2** COMMUNICATION FOR ACADEMIC STUDY (2)

Step 2

Work in pairs and discuss the question below.

When do you speak to others directly? When indirectly? Why? (Please explain your answers with the examples in your daily life.)

Results of your discussion

Speaking directly or indirectly

Listen to the conversations and fill in the blanks.

1. Adolfo and Tri are classmates.

    Adolfo: Excuse me, Tri. Did you bring your book today?

    Tri: Yes, I did. _____?

    Adolfo: I forgot my book today, and we're going to review for the quiz. _____ sharing your book with me while we do the review?

2. Richard(R) and Sandra(S) are officemates.

    R: Hi, Sandra.

    S: Hi, Richard.

    R: How are you doing?

Module 3 Speaking Directly or Indirectly

   S: I'm OK, but _____, I'm _____ irritated. You took the computer out of the office yesterday for your seminar, and I was stuck here with no computer. _____ let me know in the future if you want to take the computer out of the office.

3. Mr. Sarkes(S) and Ms. Arawan(A) are negotiating at a peace conference.

   Ms. A: Well, Mr. Sarkis, that's what we can offer you. I think you'll agree that it is a very generous offer. So perhaps we can sign the agreement now?

   Mr. S: _____ more time to speak with our council members about these negotiations before we reach a final decision.

4. Lucia(L) and Christina(C) are business partners.

   L: This proposal is ready to be signed. I'm glad we finished it before the end of the week.

   C: Me too! That was a lot of work, but I think we did a good job.

   L: Yes, I think so too. Listen, _____ the final revisions while I go to meet with the sales team.

5. Bill(B) and Sonja(S) are in the same cohort group.

   B: Well, the group is almost finished with this project, but we're still waiting for the data that you were supposed to gather.

   S: Yes, I know, _____, and I'm feeling really overloaded right now.

   B: _____ this project is due very soon. We could sure use those statistics by Friday _____ we don't miss the deadline.

Step 2

Listen to the conversations again, and discuss the questions with your partner.

1. What do you think about the speakers' speech in the conversations? Direct or indirect?

BRIDGE TO COLLEGE
交流与表达 2 COMMUNICATION FOR ACADEMIC STUDY (2)

2. Which speech sounds polite? Direct or indirect speech?
3. According to the conversations, when/To whom will you use direct or indirect speech?
4. Do you think the direct speech in English is the same as that in Chinese? Why?

 **ACTIVITY 3** ▶

Understanding directly/indirectly speaking and politeness

Analyze the following situations with your partners and figure out which expression(s) is/are used appropriately.

Situation 1

A native English-speaking student uses a lot of slang. You are not familiar with the slang, and you cannot understand it.

A. "You should use words everyone understands."
B. "I'm not quite sure what that means."

Situation 2

A student in class feels that the class is not satisfying his needs. Perhaps the material is too easy, or the student is not sure what the purpose of the lesson is.

A. "This material is really boring."
B. "I'm really unhappy in this class."
C. "I'm not sure I understand… Would you mind explaining?"
D. "I think I might learn more if…"

Module 3　Speaking Directly or Indirectly

Step 2

Discuss with your partners, and figure out the relationship between speaking directly/indirectly and politeness.

Results of your discussion

TASK TWO
Expressing Yourself Directly or Indirectly

Expressing yourself indirectly

Watch the video and write down the information that is important to you.

The important information

BRIDGE TO COLLEGE
交流与表达 2 COMMUNICATION FOR ACADEMIC STUDY (2)

Work in pairs and make a list of expressions related to expressing oneself indirectly.

Useful expressions for speaking indirectly

ASSIGNMENTS

Work in pairs and make a conversation with the situations given below.

Situation 1

If your roommate borrowed 500 yuan from you but he hasn't return the money for a long time, what are you going to say to him?

Situation 2

If your friend invites you to visit someone whom you don't like, what are you going to say?

Module 4 Making Direct or Indirect Suggestions

Module 4 Making Direct or Indirect Suggestions

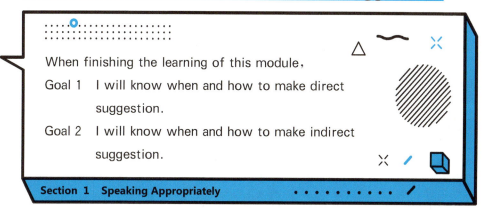

When finishing the learning of this module,
Goal 1 I will know when and how to make direct suggestion.
Goal 2 I will know when and how to make indirect suggestion.

Section 1 Speaking Appropriately

TASK ONE
Making Direct or Indirect Suggestion

Warming up

Work in pairs and discuss the questions below.

1. To whom do you give your advice or suggestions? Your fellows, your parents or your teachers? Why?
2. If you want to give your parents or teachers a suggestion, how do you say to them? Direct or indirect? Would you like to give an example? Or do you have

any other ways to show your suggestions? Or do you keep silent and hide your suggestions in your heart?

Recognizing different types of suggestions

Listen to the conversations and note down the speakers' advice.

Hiro Yakumura is always sick. What should he do?

His friend's advice: _____.

His mother's advice: _____.

His doctor's advice: _____.

Step 2

Listen to the conversations again, and discuss the questions with your partner.

Can you figure out the different ways of expressing the advice by different people in the listening? Could you explain? Summarize the different types of suggestions in English.

Results of your discussion

Module 4 Making Direct or Indirect Suggestions

Step 3

Study and read aloud the information box below.

⇒ **Making polite and indirect suggestions**
- Don't you think we should…?
- If I were you, I'd….
- Have you thought about…?
- Shall we…?
- Why don't we/you…?
- You can/could….

⇒ **Making friendly and direct suggestions**
- Why not…?
- How/What about…?
- Do…, please!

⇒ **Making strong advice**
- You'd better….
- You must….
- You should/ought to/have to….

Step 4

Work in groups of 3 or 4 and discuss the following questions.

1. When/To whom will you use the three types of suggestions?
2. What's the difference of using "Do…!" and "Do…, please!"? Which one is a proper expression when you speak to your close friend?

BRIDGE TO COLLEGE
交流与表达 2　COMMUNICATION FOR ACADEMIC STUDY (2)

Results of your discussion

 **ACTIVITY 3** ▶

Understanding the proper uses of different types of suggestions

Step 1

Work in groups of 3 or 4 and compare the following two cases to answer the questions below.

Case 1

Professor Pearce came to China for a conference. He left for the U. S. through Macau (澳门). After crossing the border, he noticed a sign in both Chinese and English that read: *"Passengers with bulky hand baggage or who are disabled or infirm must use the lift."* He shrugged and said to a Chinese standing next to him, "Does this mean kindness or discrimination?" The Chinese said, "I think this is a case of poor translation. It means kindness in Chinese."

Case 2

Module 4　Making Direct or Indirect Suggestions

Questions

1. Why did professor Pearce feel confused with the friendly reminder?
2. How do you improve the sign in Case 1?

Results of your discussion

TASK TWO
Making Suggestions in a Proper Way

Making suggestions appropriately

Watch the video and write down the information that is important to you.

Important information

BRIDGE TO COLLEGE
交流与表达 2 COMMUNICATION FOR ACADEMIC STUDY (2)

Step 2

Work in pairs and discuss the question: In what kind of situations you will make suggestions in the way shown in the video?

Results of your discussion

ASSIGNMENTS

Work in pairs and make a conversation with the situations given below.

Situation 1

Please give a suggestion to any of your teachers, so that you can learn better.

Situation 2

If your roommate is always absent from the class, what are you going to say to him?

Situation 3

If you are asked to give a piece of advice to your fellows who are still in their high school, what are you going to say?

Module 5 Making a Polite Request

Module 5 Making a Polite Request

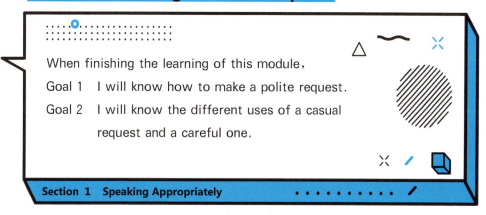

When finishing the learning of this module,
Goal 1 I will know how to make a polite request.
Goal 2 I will know the different uses of a casual request and a careful one.

Section 1 Speaking Appropriately

TASK ONE
Making a Polite Request

Warming up

Work in pairs and analyze the following case.

> Jeff was pleased to have been assigned an international student as his roommate Li Ming in his second year at a small liberal arts college in the U. S. Li Ming was an easy-going guy, a good listener, warm-hearted, and

always ready for a new experience. He appreciated Jeff's explanations of American life in an unfamiliar language. Jeff didn't think Li Ming was any more difficult to get along with than the American roommate he had the year before, except that he seemed to want to study more than Jeff was used to and he sometimes borrowed Jeff's things without asking first.

One night Jeff was working on a project that required some artwork. Li Ming was at his desk studying for a test. Jeff's scissors were just too dull to do the job, so he asked Li Ming, *"Sorry to bother you while you're studying, but could I use your scissors for a while?"* Li Ming said, "Sure," opened his desk drawer and handed Jeff the scissors. "Thanks, thanks a lot," Jeff said.

A few minutes later Jeff decided that his crayons were not going to do the trick. He addressed his roommate again: *"Sorry to bug you again, but these crayons make this look like kindergarten. You know those colored pencils you have? Would it be OK if I used them for my project?"* Li Ming got up and got them off the shelf and said, "Help yourself," and went back to reading as Jeff thanked him.

After another few minutes, Jeff said, *"I must be driving you crazy, but have you got any glue or tape? Promise I'll buy you another roll."* Li Ming handed Jeff a roll of tape that was on his desk saying, "Use as much as you want. I don't need it." "Appreciate it," mumbled Jeff as he went back to his project. Li Ming went back to his reading.

As Jeff was finishing his project he noticed that Li Ming was watching him. He looked up and was surprised to hear his Chinese roommate ask him in a plaintive tone, <u>*"Are you angry at me?"*</u>

"Of course not," Jeff replied, "what makes you think that?"

Question What makes Li Ming think Jeff is mad at him?

Module 5 Making a Polite Request

Make a polite request

Compare the following two conversations, and explain any cultural differences you found in them. Student A is a foreign student; Student B is an English native speaker.

Situation 1 Borrow a pen from your close teacher (Prof. John Smith).

Student A	Student B
A: Excuse me. Prof.: Yes? A: Can I borrow your pen? Prof.: Sure. Here you go. A: Thank you. Prof.: No problem.	B: Excuse me, Professor. Prof.: Yes? B: I forgot my pen today … do you happen to have an extra one? Prof.: Yes, as a matter of fact I do. Here you go. B: Thank you. Prof.: You're welcome.

Cultural differences I found

BRIDGE TO COLLEGE
交流与表达 2 COMMUNICATION FOR ACADEMIC STUDY (2)

Situation 2 Make an appointment to see **your tutor** (Prof. John Smith) in order to **ask about your study**.

Student A	Student B
A: Hi, John. Prof.: Hi, Tom. How are you doing? A: Fine, thank you. How are you? Prof.: Good. A: Ah, I'm now doing my writing, and I want you to correct this. Prof.: Sure. A: So can I have an appointment? Prof.: You can come anytime during my office hours tomorrow. A: Really? Prof.: Yeah. A: Uh, I'll be at 3 o'clock tomorrow. Prof.: Sounds good to me. A: Okay. Prof.: See you then. A: Thank you. See you.	B: Excuse me, Professor Smith. Prof: Yes? B: I had a question about the homework, and I was wondering if I could stop by and see, uh, see you in your office sometime? Prof.: Yeah, uh, my office hours are tomorrow from three to four. So… B: Okay, so I should stop by then? Prof.: Yeah. B: Okay, thanks a lot. See you then. Prof.: See you tomorrow.

Cultural differences I found

Module 5 Making a Polite Request

Step 2

Read the cases of the native speaker in Step 1 again. Work in pairs and figure out some strategies for making a polite request.

1. Polite requests are often more _____ and _____er.

   Direct strategies
   (1) Giving an order
       Close the window.
   (2) Showing that a speaker is requesting or expressing willingness
       I would like to ask you to close the window.
   (3) Showing speaker's desire
       I want you to close the window.
       I would appreciate it if you could close the window.

   Indirect strategies
   (1) Suggesting
       How about closing the window?
   (2) Asking about a hearer's ability
       Can you / could you close the window?
       Will you / would you close the window?
       Would you mind closing the window?
   (3) Hints
       You have *left* the window open…
       It's cold *here*.

2. Discourse structures for requests

   A *casual* request
   (1) Getting attention
   (2) (Supportive sentences)
   (3) Requesting
   (4) Thanking

   A *careful* request
   (1) Getting attention
   (2) (Small talk)
   (3) **Supportive sentences**
       e. g. _____
   (4) **Requesting with modifications**
       e. g. _____
   (5) Thanking
   (6) (Closing a conversation)

3. Techniques for softening the force of the request

   (1) Change of grammatical choices. Work in pairs and figure out what grammar is used in the polite requests below.

   (Question) <u>Can</u> you pass me the salt? (*vs.* Pass me the salt.)

   (Negative question) <u>Can't</u> you pass me the salt?

   (   ) Could you pass me the salt? (*vs.* Can you pass me the salt?)

   (   ) I am wondering if you could mail this for me. (*vs.* I wonder if…)

   (   ) I wanted to ask you about this. (*vs.* I want to ask you…)

   (   ) I was wondering if you couldn't mail this for me.

   (2) Softening words and phrases. Please fill in the brackets with the softening words or phrases.

   Clean your room, (   ).

   Clean your room (   ) (   ) before dinner.

   Could you (   ) lend me your book?

   Do you (   ) I could borrow your book? →

   Do you (   ) if I borrowed your phone? →

   (   ) (   ) (   ) OK if you help me?

   I (   ) (   ) if you could write it for me.

Module 5　Making a Polite Request

"Help Me Out"

In the schedule below, write five tasks you plan to do but need help with, e.g. washing the car, cleaning the house, etc.

Date	Morning	Afternoon	Evening
Monday			
Tuesday			
Wednesday			
Thursday			
Friday			
Saturday			
Sunday			

Make requests and find classmates who are free to help you with your five tasks.

Directions If a classmate agrees to your request, have them sign their name in the square under the activity. Also, fill in the rest of the schedule with tasks that your classmate have asked you for help with. If you are free at a stated day and time, accept the request and write the task information in the schedule. If you already have something to do, decline the request and give your reason.

Making a request	Accepting a request	Declining a request
Can/Could you…?	Of course.	I'm sorry. That's no possible.
Would you mind…?	Certainly.	I'm afraid not.
Would you be free/willing to…?	Yes, that's no problem at all.	I'm afraid that's just not possible at the moment.
…	No problem.	…
	…	

ASSIGNMENTS

Work in pairs and make a conversation with the situations given below.

Situation 1

You have recently moved to a new apartment. Because it is very far from campus, you need to buy a used car as soon as possible. However, since you have never bought a car by yourself, you want **your close American friend** (**Peter**) to go and find a good, affordable used car with you. What do you do?

Situation 2

You are planning to apply to several undergraduate programs in order to study (   ). Therefore, you have to ask **your professor** to write a letter of recommendation for you to these programs. **You know him well and are taking his class now.** What do you say?

Module 6 Making a Serious and Formal Invitation

Module 6 Making a Serious and Formal Invitation

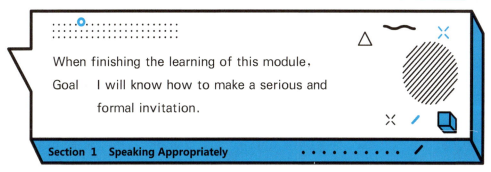

Goal: When finishing the learning of this module, I will know how to make a serious and formal invitation.

Section 1 Speaking Appropriately

Warming up

Work in pairs and discuss the questions.

1. How do you know an invitation in Chinese culture is formal?
2. How do you know an invitation in Chinese culture is serious?

Results of your discussion

BRIDGE TO COLLEGE
交流与表达 2 COMMUNICATION FOR ACADEMIC STUDY (2)

 **ACTIVITY 2**

Understanding a formal invitation

Watch the two video clips and fill in the blanks.

Video clip 1

Peter: That's been a tremendous help, Jens. Really helped clarify things. We'll get these proposals off to the agency, see what they have to say about it. Could you help with that, Maria?

Maria: Certainly.

Peter: Puala will show you how. Now, I must rush. I've got another meeting.

Jens: (to Maria) Promotion!

Peter: Oh, _____ pop round _____. _____?
_____?

Jens: _____ ...

Peter: (to Maria) _____?

Maria: _____ ... _____?

Peter: If that's all right with you. Right, I must rush. See you later.

Maria: What does he mean, "pop round"?

Jens: Probably tea. You know how the English love to "pop round" for tea. I'm only joking. I suppose it means dinner.

Maria: _____?

Jens: I don't know. Eight o'clock? Look like we've been honoured.
_____?

Video clip 2

Peter: That's been a tremendous help, Jens. Really helped to clarify things. We'll get these proposals off to the agency, see what they have to say. Can you help with that, Maria?

Module 6 Making a Serious and Formal Invitation

Maria: Certainly.
Peter: Paula will show you how. I've got to go, I'm afraid. I've got another meeting.
Jens: (to Maria) Promotion!
Peter: Oh, by the way, _____ want to invite you to dinner one day this week. _____, if that suits you?
Maria: _____.
Peter: _____. _____. Just the four of us. My wife's very much looking forward to meeting you both.
Maria: That sounds nice. _____?
Peter: No, not far. Best to take a taxi, though. Right, I must be going. See you later.
Jens: _____?
Peter: That's right. See you tomorrow.
Maria: That's a surprise.
Jens: Yes. I've got a car with me. I could give you a lift, if you like?
Maria: That would be nice.
Jens: _____?
Maria: Daphne.

Step 2

Compare the two video clips. Please find out what is wrong in making an invitation in the first video clip, and figure out how to make a formal invitation in the second clip.

Problems I found

037

BRIDGE TO COLLEGE

交流与表达 2　COMMUNICATION FOR ACADEMIC STUDY (2)

Proper ways to make a serious invitation

 ACTIVITY 3 ▶

Understanding how to make a serious invitation.

Listen to the passage and write down the important information you think.

The important information

Check your notes with a partner.

Module 6　Making a Serious and Formal Invitation

Step 3

Listen and have a dictation of the conversations. Then decide whether they are serious invitations or not.

Conversation 1

Conversation 2

Conversation 3

Conversation 4

BRIDGE TO COLLEGE
交流与表达 2 COMMUNICATION FOR ACADEMIC STUDY (2)

Module 7 Accepting or Declining an Invitation

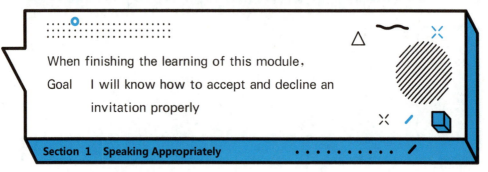

Goal: When finishing the learning of this module, I will know how to accept and decline an invitation properly

Section 1 Speaking Appropriately

Warming up

Listen to a story once and answer the questions.

1. Where does the story take place?
2. What was the man thinking about?

Your answers

Module 7　Accepting or Declining an Invitation

Step 2

Listen to the story at the barber shop three times, and have a dictation.

Possible vocabulary

manicure 护甲/美甲　　　　　　　shave 剃须

Your dictation

Step 3

Work in pairs and answer the questions.

- What words did the man use to invite the girl?
- Did the girl accept or refuse his invitation?
- How did the girl respond?

BRIDGE TO COLLEGE
交流与表达 2 COMMUNICATION FOR ACADEMIC STUDY (2)

 **ACTIVITY 2** ▶

Understanding how to accept/decline an invitation

Listen to a dialogue, fill in the blanks and figure out how to accept an invitation.

Diarmuid: _____?

Catherine: Er, I'm not sure yet. _____?

Diarmuid: OK, well I'm going to have a dinner party at my house and _____
_____.

Catherine: Oh right, yes, _____. _____?

Diarmuid: No, it's just a few old friends really. You'll… you'll… you'll have a good time, you'll like the people. _____?

Catherine: That'd be lovely. _____?

Diarmuid: Oh I think so…!

Catherine: OK then!

Step 2

Work in pairs and fill in the blanks, then discuss how to decline an invitation.

A: Are you free on Friday?

B: I'm not sure. Why?

A: I have two tickets for *Avengers: Infinity War*. Would you like to go with me?

B: Oh, I'm afraid _____, because _____.

A: That sounds terrible, but I can understand.

B: How about _____?

A: OK!

Module 7 Accepting or Declining an Invitation

* **The elements of making a formal invitation**

  Pre-invitation: *What are you doing on Friday, Catherine?*

  Invitation: *I would very much like it if you could come along.*

  Accepting/declining: *Yes, I'd love to. / I'm sorry*

  Etiquette: *Shall I bring a bottle?*

* **Accepting an invitation**

  - **Great. I'll give you a call.**
  - **OK. I'll call you.**
  - **That sounds good.**
  - **Sure. Good idea.**

  ➡

  - **What time** …?
  - **Where?**
  - **Can I bring** …?
  - **Should we dress formally?**

* **Declining an invitation**

  - I' sorry.
  - I can't make it then.
  - That's bad time for me.
  - I'm busy that day.
  - No, …

  ➡

  - Maybe another day?
  - But let's get together soon.

Step 3

Practice inviting someone to do something by the following procedure.

1. Think about what words can you use to invite someone to do something.

   Are you free …

   Would you like to …

2. Think about what you can invite someone to do.

   play tennis

   go to a movie

   …

3. Think about what people say when they say "yes" to an invitation.

   I'd love to.

   That sounds great.

   ...

4. Think about what reasons people give when they say "no" to an invitation.

   I have to work.

   I already have plans.

   ...

5. Now sit with a partner. Practice inviting someone to do something, and practice saying "yes" and "no".

ASSIGNMENTS

Work in pairs and make a conversation with the situations given below.

Situation 1

You are the leader of the Student Union. You are inviting Mr. ×××, **the school master of your school**, to attend a very important meeting and give a speech.

Situation 2

You are inviting your roommates to do something with you. One of them accepts, but the other one refuses.

Module 8 Making Apologies

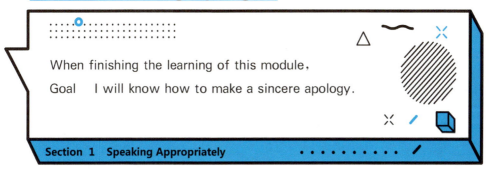

When finishing the learning of this module,
Goal   I will know how to make a sincere apology.

Section 1 Speaking Appropriately

Warming up

Read the dialogue below and underline the expressions of complaint and highlight the expressions of apology.

Agent: Good morning. Can I help you?

Mr. Williams: We'd like to make a complaint about our holiday in Portugal last week.

Agent: I'm sorry to hear that. What exactly was the problem?

Mr. Williams: First of all the coach taking us us to the hotel broke down and we had to wait for over two hours before a replacement arrived. Then when we got the hotel we found our room hadn't been cleaned.

Agent: Oh dear, did you complain to the hotel staff?

Mr. Williams: Of course, but they told us that the chambermaids were on strike. Anyway, that's not all. The people in the room upstairs were having all-night parties, and every night. I demanded another room but the receptionist told me the hotel was full.

Agent: Oh, I see.

Mr. Williams: And we were dissatisfied with the food in the hotel restaurant, too. It was so bad we had to eat out all the time despite having paid for meals in the price of our holiday.

Agent: I do apologize. I'd like to offer you a 20% discount on the price of one of our Autumn breaks as a gesture of goodwill.

Read the following expressions and sort them into the right column:

— Please forgive me for…
— Excuse me, but there is a problem with…
— Sorry to bother you, but there is something wrong with…
— I deeply regret what I did/said.
— I'm afraid I have to complain about…
— There is really no excuse for what I did/said.
— I must beg your pardon.
— I'm sorry to have to say this, but…
— Please accept my sincere apology for…
— I have had enough of…

Complaint	Apology

Module 8   Making Apologies

 ACTIVITY 2 ▶

Understanding how to make an effective apology

Read the information box below.

Apologizing and Responding

Formal Apologies
- I'm (awfully/terribly) sorry about
- I'm sorry that …
- I owe you an apology.
- I apologize for …
- I'd like to apologize for …
- Please, forgive me for my …
- Please, accept my apologies for …

Response
- That's quite all right.
- Please don't worry about it.
- I accept your apology.

Informal Apologies
- I'm really sorry about …
- Sorry for …
- I hope you aren't mad about …
- Excuse me for …
- Pardon me for this, …

Response
- That's OK.
- Never mind.
- Forget about it.
- I doesn't matter.
- You couldn't help it.
- No harm done.

Accepting responsibility
- I promise it won't happen again.
- I'll be more careful next time.
- It's all my fault.

BRIDGE TO COLLEGE
交流与表达 2   COMMUNICATION FOR ACADEMIC STUDY (2)

Work in pairs and discuss the following situations based on what you have learned from Step 1.

In which of these situations would people expect you to apologize? What would you say?

— When you arrive after the appointed time of a meeting
— When you telephone someone after 10 p.m.
— When you have forgotten something you were expected to bring
— When you walk into someone accidentally
— When you break something which does not belong to you
— When you unintentionally offend someone

Put the following conversations into the correct order.

Conversation 1

___ A: Could we possibly reschedule our appointment for tomorrow morning?

___ A: Sure. I apologize again for this morning. I promise it won't happen again.

___ A: I'm terribly sorry, Sir, that I missed our meeting this morning. The reason was that my car wouldn't start and I had trouble getting to work.

___ B: All right. Let's try for tomorrow morning. Same time, same place?

___ B: Well, don't worry about it. I understand, but we still need to meet to discuss the budget concerns.

Conversation 2

___ A: But, I still feel that I owe you an apology and an explanation. We were all talking about politics and I didn't realize that you didn't want to talk

Module 8 Making Apologies

about the last election in your country. I'm sorry I involved you in the conversation.

____ A: I hope you aren't mad about last night. I didn't mean to ask you any embarrassing questions about your country. I'm sorry.

____ B: It's OK. Don't worry about it.

____ B: Don't worry about it. It's forgotten.

Conversation 3

____ A: I hope it won't leave a stain. I'm awfully sorry.

____ A: here let me help you. I didn't realize that glass was so full. When I turned around, I spilled the wine.

____ B: It will be OK.

____ B: Don't worry. I will get it out.

____ B: Accidents happen. Please don't worry about it.

Step 4

Study the conversations in Step 3. Figure out the strategies to make an effective apology and write down more expressions related to the certain strategy.

⇒ **Apologizing**

　— Oh, I'm sorry about that.

　_____

　— My apologies…

　_____

　— I apologize for the inconvenience…

　_____

⇒ _____

　— This was because…

　_____

— Unfortunately, this was unavoidable as
  _____

— The main reason for this was…
  _____

⇒ **Accepting responsibility**

— It's all my fault.
  _____

⇒ _____

— Could we possibly reschedule the meeting?
  _____

Step 5

Work in pairs and make conversations with the following situations provided.

Situation 1

You go to a concert and want to get to your seat, but a person is blocking the aisle and some people are waiting behind you.

Situation 2

You are in class but don't feel well. You decide that you have no choice but to leave early even though the professor is in the middle of the lecture.

Situation 3

Partner A: Your friend had a birthday party last night. You have promised him to go but you didn't. It was because you had a bad headache at that time. Today you meet him on the way home from work. Apologize to him sincerely.

Partner B: You and your other friends had been waiting for him for a long time. You are a bit disappointed. After listening to his explanation, you think that's OK.

Module 8 Making Apologies

ASSIGNMENTS

Listen to "BBC 6 minutes—Punctuality & Apology", and note down the important information you think.

> The important information

SECTION 2

Communicating in Daily Life

Module 9　Finding the Right Words to Express Yourself

Module 9　Finding the Right Words to Express Yourself

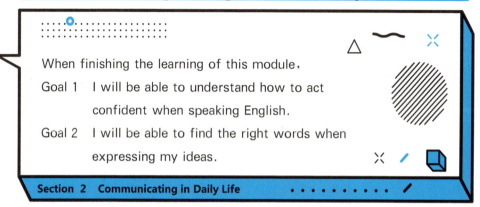

When finishing the learning of this module,
Goal 1　I will be able to understand how to act confident when speaking English.
Goal 2　I will be able to find the right words when expressing my ideas.

Section 2　Communicating in Daily Life

TASK ONE
Understanding How to Act Confident When Speaking English

Listen to the audio and write down the information as required below. You will hear the recording three times.

◇ Topic of this listening: _____

Problems	Solutions

BRIDGE TO COLLEGE
交流与表达 2 COMMUNICATION FOR ACADEMIC STUDY (2)

Share the notes with your partner and complement each other's information.

TASK TWO
Finding the Right Words

We all know how important vocabulary is when we are learning a language. Finding the exact words for the idea you want to express is important for becoming a fluent, confident speaker. It is not unusual for learners of English to feel that they don't know enough words. Do you have the same problem? How do you solve the problem?

Read the case and discuss the questions in groups of 3 or 4.

Case

One of Xiao Ming's problems is his spoken English. Sometimes when he tries to say something but he can't find the exact word, he feels a bit anxious and stops there because he doesn't know how to express himself. As a result, he feels less confident in speaking and thus he stops himself from speaking sometimes.

Module 9 Finding the Right Words to Express Yourself

1. Could you figure out Xiao Ming's problem in speaking? What is that?
2. What suggestions do you have to solve his problem?

Results of your discussion

Step 2

Carefully read the information box below. Highlight the very important information.

Not having a wide vocabulary can have a serious effect on your confidence as a speaker. How can you become more confident even if you don't know a lot of words. Here are some suggestions:

1. Explain what you mean. Don't worry if you can't find the exact word you are searching for. Instead, try to explain what you mean. This is known as **paraphrasing** and is an important skill. You can give a short definition-for example, if you forget the word "envelope", you might say "the thing you put a letter in before you post it". Or you can give a description. So, instead of "elephant" you could say "a big, grey animal with large ears. They live in Africa." You can even use your hands to demonstrate the meaning.

2. Start your sentence again. If you simply stop when you reach a word you don't know, the person who is listening to you will just stop listening. Remember that what you are saying is important to you and to them. To give yourself more time to think of a word or definition, go back to the beginning of your sentence and start again. It's not unusual to hear native speakers of English say "What was I saying?" before repeating what they've said. Remember: try to give yourself time to think.

BRIDGE TO COLLEGE
交流与表达 2 COMMUNICATION FOR ACADEMIC STUDY (2)

> **3. Ask for help.** If you get stuck and really can't think of the word you need, why not ask the person listening for help? You could say "I can't think of the word I need". Together, you and your listener might be able to find the words for the idea you want to express. Working together with the person who is listening will make life easier for you and give you both a chance to practise speaking and listening.

Step 3

Work in pairs. Think of three words or phrases in Chinese which you don't know how to say them in English. Try to think of a definition or explanation for each word or phrase in English. Then explain them to your partner to see if they can identify the word or phrase from your explanation.

Step 4

Work in pairs. Partner A will get a topic from your teacher and talk about it without preparation. When Partner A finished his/her work, Partner B will get another topic from the teacher and talk about it at once. When you do the oral practice, you may follow suggestions mentioned in the information box just in case you don't know how to say an exact word during your speech.

⇒ Time limit: two minutes/each person
⇒ Teacher will be the time-keeper.
⇒ If necessary, you can read the information box again in two minutes.

Module 9 Finding the Right Words to Express Yourself

ASSIGNMENTS

Watch the video "Airport Vocabulary" and note down the words and expressions. Translate them into Chinese.

BRIDGE TO COLLEGE
交流与表达 2　COMMUNICATION FOR ACADEMIC STUDY（2）

Module 10　Airport or Railway Station

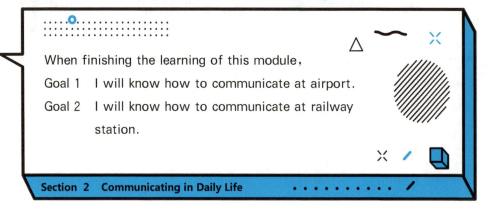

When finishing the learning of this module,
Goal 1　I will know how to communicate at airport.
Goal 2　I will know how to communicate at railway station.

Section 2　Communicating in Daily Life

PRE-TASK

- List what you have to do at the airport.
    - Check in
    - ...
- List what you have to do at the railway station.

Module 10　Airport or Railway Station

TASK ONE
Learning How to Communicate at Airport

ACTIVITY 1 ▶

Check-in

Step 1

Fill in the blanks.

Situation 1

You are at the airport check-in desk. You are flying from Xi'an to Yantai in Shandong Province.

Agent: Good afternoon! Where are you flying to today?

You: (1) _____.

Agent: May I have your (2) _____?

You: Here you go.

Agent: Are you checking any bags?

You: Just this one.

Agent: OK, please (3) _____ your bag on the scale.

You: I have a stopover in Jinan—do I need to pick up my luggage there?

Agent: No, it'll go straight through to Yantai. Here are your boarding passes—your flight leaves from (4) _____ 15A and it'll begin boarding at 3:20. Your (5) _____ is 26E.

You: Thanks.

BRIDGE TO COLLEGE
交流与表达 2 COMMUNICATION FOR ACADEMIC STUDY (2)

Situation 2

You are at the airport check-in desk. You are flying from Beijing to New York City.

You: Hi.

Agent: Good morning. What's your final destination?

You: New York City.

Agent: May I see your (1) _____, please?

You: Certainly. Here you are.

Agent: Would you like a window seat or an aisle seat?

You: A window seat, please.

Agent: Could you place your bag on the luggage belt, please?

You: Sure!

Agent: Did you pack it yourself?

You: Yes.

Agent: Has your luggage been in your possession at all times? / Has your luggage been outside your supervision (or possession) at any time

You: (2) _____ / _____.

Agent: Has anyone given you anything to carry on the flight?

You: (3) _____.

Agent: Do you have any firearms, hazardous materials or liquids in your bag?

You: (4) _____.

Agent: Are you aware of the regulations regarding liquids in your carry-on, which must be 3.4 ounces or less and placed inside a single quart-sized transparent plastic bag?

You: Yes.

Agent: Oh, I'm afraid your bag has exceeded the maximum baggage allowance, so you'll have to pay the excess baggage charge.

You: Oh, right.

Module 10 Airport or Railway Station

Agent: If you just go over to that counter over there, you can pay the amount. Then, just come back here with the receipt and I'll put your (5) _____ straight through.

You: OK. Thanks. [Ten minutes later, you come back and hand her the receipt.] Here you are.

Agent: Thank you. Here's your boarding (6) _____. Your flight leaves at 13:34. Boarding will commence at 12:45. The boarding gate hasn't been announced yet, but it should appear on the flight information (7) _____ in about half an hour. The security check-in area is just over there. Have a nice flight!

You: Thanks.

Find a partner and role play the conversations in the two situations.

Going through security

Step 1

Translate the underlined sentences into Chinese.

Agent: (1) <u>Please lay your bags flat on the conveyor belt, and use the bins for small objects.</u>

You: Do I need to take my laptop out of the bag?

Agent: Yes, you do. Take off your hat and your shoes, too.

(you walk through the metal detector)

[BEEP BEEP BEEP BEEP]

Agent: Please step back. (2) <u>Do you have anything in your pockets-keys, cell phone, loose change?</u>

You: I don't think so. Let me try taking off my belt.

Agent: Okay, (3) <u>come on through.</u>

(you go through the metal detector again)

Agent: (4) <u>You're all set!</u> Have a nice flight.

Find a partner and role play the conversation.

Listening to the information at the gate

Airports are divided into terminals (the major sections of the airport) and each terminal has many gates. The gate is the door you go through to enter the airplane. Here are a few announcements you might hear while you are at the gate, waiting for the plane to board.

Module 10 Airport or Railway Station

Work in pairs. Read aloud your information to your partner and ask him/her to repeat the information. When he/she finishes the retelling, give him/her the reminder(s) related to the information. Before sharing the information and reminders, you two will have 10 minutes to read them.

For Partner A

Information	Reminders
"Attention passengers of United Airlines flight 880. There has been a gate change. United Airlines flight 880 will now be leaving from gate 12."	Know your flight number in English, so that you can pay attention to the announcement and know if you need to go to a different gate.
"United Airlines flight 880 to Miami is now boarding."	This means it's time for passengers to enter the plane.
"We would like to invite our first-and business-class passengers, Star Club Premium members, and passengers requiring special assistance to board at gate 12."	This means that passengers who are "special" (first class, business class, or in the Star Club) or passengers who are elderly (old), disabled, pregnant, or with small children can go into the airplane FIRST.
"We would now like to invite all passengers seated in Zone/Group 1—that's rows 1-16—to begin boarding United Airlines flight 880 at gate 12."	This means that passengers of economic class will be asked to board group by group. Look at your boarding pass to know your "zone number" and what "row" your seat number is.

BRIDGE TO COLLEGE
交流与表达 2　COMMUNICATION FOR ACADEMIC STUDY (2)

For Partner B

Information	Tips
"We would now like to invite all passengers to board United Airlines flight 880 to Miami at gate 12."	This means the number of passengers is not very large, so everyone can enter the plane.
"This is the last call for United Airlines flight 880 to Miami, now boarding at gate number 12."	This means it is the FINAL OPPORTUNITY to enter the plane before they close the doors.
"Passenger John Smith. Passenger John Smith, please proceed to the United Airlines desk at gate 12."	Sometimes the announcement will call a specific passenger by name. The word "proceed" in this context is a formal way to say "go." The reason is that the passengers the stand-by passengers. On most modern airlines, flying standby occurs when a passenger travels on a flight without a prior reservation for that specific flight. There are four circumstances in which passengers typically fly standby. First, a missed flight may require a passenger to fly standby on the next flight to the same destination, as they now lack a reservation. Secondly, a passenger may arrive at the airport early (whether accidentally or on purpose) and wish to take an earlier flight listed for that day. They will then attempt to travel standby on the earlier flight, and failing that, proceed to take their booked flight. This is referred to in the industry as "go-show".

Module 10 Airport or Railway Station

"Passenger John Smith. Passenger John Smith, please proceed to the United Airlines desk at gate 12."	Standby can also occur for upgrades. Many airlines (particularly in the United States) give free space available domestic upgrades to First Class for their elite tier fliers. If first class sells out or upgrades full with higher-tiered passengers, elite fliers can standby for a first class seat, should one open up due to a cancellation, no-show, misconnect, irregular operations or an equipment change. If a passenger clears for an upgrade, they may be given new boarding passes at the gate. Some airlines, such as American and United, have gateside monitors that show the upgrade (as well as general) standby list, and will also announce when First Class checks in full (i.e., no further upgrades will be given). In some cases, when a flight compartment is overbooked, an airline will designate all passengers who do not have a seat assignment as "standby" at some time prior to boarding.

BRIDGE TO COLLEGE
交流与表达 2 COMMUNICATION FOR ACADEMIC STUDY (2)

TASK TWO
Learning How to Communicate at Railway/Underground Station

Getting information at the tube/underground station

You are a tourist in London. You want to get to Waterloo Station.

Fill in the blanks in the conversation below.

You: Hi. Do you think you could help me, please?

Agent: Yes, sure.

You: I'm trying to get to Waterloo Station. (1) _____（去那里最好的方式是什么?）

Agent: Probably by tube.

You: OK. Do you know which (2) _____ it is?

Agent: Yes, it's the er, the Northern Line.

You: Great. And (3) _____（你知道最近的地铁站在哪里吗?）

Agent: Well, Covent Garden is just down this street. But then you'd have to (4) _____ at Leicester Square to get on the Northern Line. So, it'd be quicker, and easier, to walk to Leicester Square and to get the (5) _____ from there.

You: OK. That's great. Do I need to change lines after that?

Module 10 Airport or Railway Station

Agent: No, just get on a southbound (6) _____, find the platform that says "Southbound" and take the first tube that comes along. I think it's about four stops from there.

You: That's great. (7) _____.

Agent: My pleasure. Bye.

You: Bye.

Step 2

Find a partner, check your answers and role play the conversation.

Step 3

Translate the expressions into Chinese.

The expressions you will say

1. A single to Baker Street, please.
2. A return to Waterloo Station, please.
3. Which platform is it for Victoria Station, please?
4. Do I need to change lines for Waterloo Station?
5. I'd like a Travelcard, please.

The expressions you will hear

1. Stand clear of the door, please.
2. Mind the gap, please.
3. The next station is Tottenham Court Road. Change here for the Northern Line.
4. You need to take the Bakerloo line.
5. Get on the southbound train.
6. Change at Tottenham Court Road for the Northern Line.

BRIDGE TO COLLEGE
交流与表达 2 COMMUNICATION FOR ACADEMIC STUDY (2)

ASSIGNMENTS

1. Read aloud the conversations and expressions in this module. Make them yours.
2. Watch the video "English for Travel—How to Buy Tickets" and note down the useful expressions for buying tickets. Repeat after the video.
3. Work in pairs. You will get a train schedule from your teacher. You have to be ready to play the roles of both a tourist and an agent working at the ticket office. As a tourist, you are in New York City now and plans to visit GE, a well-known company at Schenectady, New York State by train. As an agent, you will be ready to help the tourist to get to the destination by train. Your work will be checked in next week's speaking class.

Module 11 Restaurants

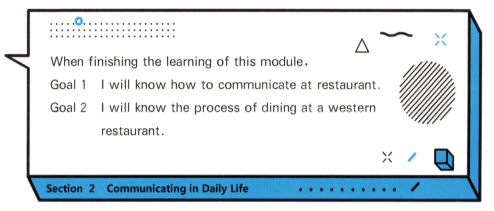

Module 11 Restaurants

When finishing the learning of this module,
Goal 1 I will know how to communicate at restaurant.
Goal 2 I will know the process of dining at a western restaurant.

Section 2 Communicating in Daily Life

PRE-TASK

Warming up

- List the process of dining at a restaurant in China.
    - ...
    - ...
    - ...

TASK ONE
Understanding the Dinning Etiquette in a Restaurant

Read the dinning etiquette in western restaurants.

- Be mindful of the proper attire.
- Wait to be seated.
- Don't leave your phone on the table.
- Put your napkin on your lap.
- Wait for everyone to be served before you start eating.
- Don't call out to your waiter.
- Treat the wait staff with respect.
- Everyone should order the same number of courses.
- Hold your wineglass by the stem.
- Leave within 15 minutes of finishing your meal.
- If you're paying the whole bill, tell the waiter in advance.
- Decide ahead of time how you're splitting the bill.
- Tip well.

Work in groups of 3 or 4 and discuss the dinning etiquette in Chinese restaurants.

Results of your discussion

Module 11 Restaurants

TASK TWO
Learning How to Communicate When Ordering the Meal

Work individually and answer the questions below.

Question 1

You are in a restaurant. You want to order something to eat. You have never heard of green salad and want to find out about it. You want to ask the waiter. What should you say?

A. Would you like a banana?

B. What is in a green salad?

C. Where is the restaurant?

Question 2

The waiter describes the green salad. You decide that you want to order one and a glass of water. What do you say?

A. I'd like a green salad and water, please.

B. I'd like a hamburger.

C. I am going to fly.

Question 3

Your host sister is at the restaurant with you. She wants you to try the cheese pizza. You don't like cheese at all. What do you say?

A. I don't like salad.

B. I like cheese.

C. No, thank you.

BRIDGE TO COLLEGE
交流与表达 2 COMMUNICATION FOR ACADEMIC STUDY (2)

Question 4

Your host sister Ella is at the restaurant with you. She wants you to try the cheese pizza. You don't like cheese at all. You say "No, thank you." Then she asks you, "Why not?" What do you say?

A. I don't like salad. It is sour.

B. I don't like cheese. It tastes nasty.

C. I don't like apple pie. It is sweet.

Step 2

Check your answers with a partner.

Step 3

Work in pairs and fill in the blanks in the conversation below.

Ping(P) and Ella(E) are at the restaurant.

E: I like hot dogs. _____（它们尝起来很美味）. Do you like apple pie?

P: No, I don't.

E: Why not?

P: I don't like sweets. _____（我喜欢辛辣的食物）.

E: I'd like the steak, a baked potato, and a green salad. _____
（我需要盐和胡椒）. I'd like a banana and some milk, too. Would you like a green salad?

P: I don't like the tomatoes. They taste nasty. I like noodles.

E: You'd like the pasta salad. It doesn't have tomatoes. Do you want some pizza?

Module 11　Restaurants

P: No, thank you. I don't like cheese.
E: _____ （你想要柠檬茶还是甜茶）?
P: I would like tea. I don't want lemon or sugar. Lemon is too sour.

Step 4

Work in pairs and fill in the missing information based on the conversations in Step 1 and Step 3 in TASK TWO.

Based on the conversations, I know that when I order my meal, I should _____.
A. express my real thoughts in a polite way.
B. hide my doubts or real thoughts to avoid offending the waiter/waitress or my host.

TASK THREE
Figuring out the Process of Dining in a Restaurant

Step 1

Watch the video clip and note down the important information you think.

Important information

Step 2

Work individually and figure out the process of dining in a restaurant based on the video and your notes. You may write down the reminders for certain step. The graph below just helps you organize your thoughts. You may not use all the boxes in it.

Steps	What you will do	Reminders
1	Wait at the entrance door to be seated.	

Step 3

Discuss your answers in a group of 3 or 4.

Module 11 Restaurants

 Step 4

Select one member to present the results of your discussion.

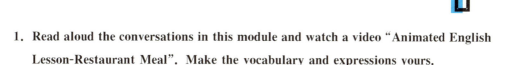

ASSIGNMENTS

1. Read aloud the conversations in this module and watch a video "Animated English Lesson-Restaurant Meal". Make the vocabulary and expressions yours.
2. Work in groups of three. You will get a menu from your teacher. You have to be ready to play the roles of waiter/waitress or guest at a restaurant. In the group, two of you will play the role of guests and the third one will play the role of waiter/waitress. You are expected to act out the whole process of ordering food. Your work should be videoed and submitted to your teacher before the next week's class.

BRIDGE TO COLLEGE
交流与表达 2 COMMUNICATION FOR ACADEMIC STUDY (2)

Module 12　Hotel

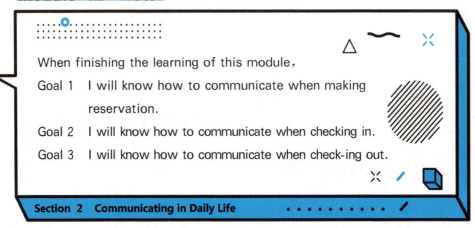

When finishing the learning of this module,
Goal 1　I will know how to communicate when making reservation.
Goal 2　I will know how to communicate when checking in.
Goal 3　I will know how to communicate when check-ing out.

Section 2　Communicating in Daily Life

PRE-TASK

- Work in groups of 3 or 4 and discuss how to book a hotel.

Results of discussion

Module 12 Hotel

TASK ONE
Making Reservation

Read the conversation and mark out the formulaic expressions about making reservation as shown in the first several lines. Underline the expressions receptionist will use and highlight the expressions client will use.

Receptionist: Good morning. Welcome to The Grand Woodward Hotel.
Client: Hi, good morning. I'd like to make a reservation for the third weekend in September. Do you have any vacancies?
R: Yes sir, we have several rooms available for that particular weekend. And what is the exact date of your arrival?
C: The 24th.
R: How long will you be staying?
C: I'll be staying for two nights.
R: How many people is the reservation for?
C: There will be two of us.
R: And would you like a room with twin beds or a double bed?
C: A double bed, please.
R: Great. And would you prefer to have a room with a view of the ocean?
C: If that type of room is available, I would love to have an ocean view. What's the rate for the room?
R: Your room is five hundred and ninety dollars per night. Now what name will the reservation be listed under?
C: Charles Hannighan.
R: Could you spell your last name for me, please?

BRIDGE TO COLLEGE
交流与表达 2 COMMUNICATION FOR ACADEMIC STUDY (2)

C: Sure. H-A-N-N-I-G-H-A-N.

R: And is there a phone number where you can be contacted?

C: Yes, my cell phone number is 555-26386.

R: Great. Now I'll need your credit card information to reserve the room for you. What type of card is it?

C: Visa. The number is 987654321.

R: And what is the name of the cardholder?

C: Charles H. Hannighan.

R: Alright, Mr. Hannighan, your reservation has been made for the twenty-fourth of September for a room with a double bed and view of the ocean. Check-in is at 2 o'clock. If you have any other questions, please do not hesitate to call us.

C: Great, thank you so much.

R: My pleasure. We'll see you in September, Mr. Hannighan. Have a nice day.

Role play the conversation with a partner.

Suppose you and your friend will have a tour in the UK. Now you are in London, and you will go to New Castle. Work with a partner and make a conversation. Your partner will play the role of receptionist at Royal Station Hotel, and you will make reservation on the phone.

In your conversation, you may use the information on the next page:

Module 12　Hotel

Price:
- Price is updated periodically and may not reflect latest room availabilities and rates.
- Current price: $69/night

Transportation from train station to hotel:
- Taxi: three minutes without heavy traffic; five minutes with heavy traffic
- Walk: two mintues

Ⓐ　Newcastle railway station
　　Neville St, Newcastle Upon Tyne NE1 5DL

↑　Depart A186 / Neville Street toward Grainger Street

↱　Turn right onto road

↰　Turn left onto road

●　Arrive at the road on the right
　　The last intersection is A186 / Neville Street

Ⓑ　Royal Station Hotel- Part Of The Cairn Collection
　　Neville Street, Newcastle Upon Tyne NE1 5DH

TASK TWO

Checking in

Step 1

Read the conversation and mark out the formulaic expressions about checking-in. Underline the expressions receptionist will use and highlight the expressions client will use.

Hotel: <u>Good afternoon. Welcome to</u> the Grand Woodward Hotel. How may I help you?

Guest: ==I have a reservation for today. It's under the name of== Hannighan.

Hotel: Can you please spell that for me, sir?

Guest: Sure. H-A-N-N-I-G-H-A-N.

Hotel: Yes, Mr. Hannighan, we've reserved a double room for you with a view of the ocean for two nights. Is that correct?

Guest: Yes, it is.

Hotel: Excellent. We already have your credit card information on file. If you'll just sign the receipt along the bottom, please.

Guest: Whoa! Five hundred and ninety dollars a night!

Hotel: Yes, sir. We are a five-star hotel after all.

Guest: Well, fine. I'm here on business anyway, so at least I'm staying on the company's dime. What's included in this cost anyway?

Hotel: A full Continental buffet every morning, free airport shuttle service, and use of the hotel's safe are all included.

Guest: So what's not included in the price?

Hotel: Well, you will find a mini-bar in your room. Any use of it will be charged to your account. Also, the hotel provides room service, at an additional charge of course.

Module 12 Hotel

Guest: Hmm. OK, so what room am I in?

Hotel: Room 487. Here is your key. To get to your room, take the elevator on the right up to the fourth floor. Turn left once you exit the elevator and your room will be on the left hand side. A bellboy will bring your bags up shortly.

Guest: Great. Thanks.

Hotel: Should you have any questions or requests, please dial "0" from your room. Also, there is internet available in the lobby 24 hours a day.

Guest: OK, and what time is check-out?

Hotel: At midday, sir.

Guest: OK, thanks.

Hotel: My pleasure, sir. Have a wonderful stay at the Grand Woodward Hotel.

Suppose you and your friend are at Royal Hotel, New Castle. Work with a partner and make a conversation about checking-in. Your partner will play the role of receptionist.

Step 3

Watch a video clip and take down more expressions about checking-in.

TASK THREE

Checking out

Step 1

Read the conversation and mark out the expressions about checking-out. Underline the expressions receptionist will use and highlight the expressions client will use.

Hotel: Did you enjoy your stay with us?

Guest: Yes, very much so. However, I now need to get to the airport. I have a flight that leaves in about two hours, so what is the quickest way to get there?

Hotel: We do have a free airport shuttle service.

Guest: That sounds great, but will it get me to the airport on time?

Hotel: Yes, it should. The next shuttle leaves in 15 minutes, and it takes approximately 25 minutes to get to the airport.

Guest: Fantastic. I'll just wait in the lounge area. Will you please let me know when it will be leaving?

Hotel: Of course, sir. Oh, before you go would you be able to settle the mini-bar bill?

Guest: Oh yes certainly. How much will that be?

Hotel: Let's see. The bill comes to $37.50. How would you like to pay for that?

Guest: I'll pay with my Visa thanks, but I'll need a receipt so I can charge it from my company.

Hotel: Absolutely. Here you are sir. If you like you can leave your bags with the porter and he can load them onto the shuttle for you when it arrives.

Guest: That would be great thank you.

Hotel: Would you like to sign the hotel guestbook too while you wait?

Guest: Sure, I had a really good stay here and I'll tell other people to come.

Hotel: That's good to hear. Thank you again for staying at The Grand Woodward Hotel.

Module 12　Hotel

Step 2

Watch a video "Check-out at a Hotel" and note down the guest's complaints and the receptionist's response.

Your notes

Step 3

Check your notes with a partner.

ASSIGNMENTS

1. Watch two videos "Real English for staying at a HOTEL" and "Travel English—Staying at a Hotel", and learn how to express when you stay at a hotel. Note down the useful expressions and translate them into Chinese.

2. Watch the video "At a Hotel—Learn English in Hamza's Classroom" to learn more expressions related to reservation and check-in. Repeat them after the video.

Module 13 Travel

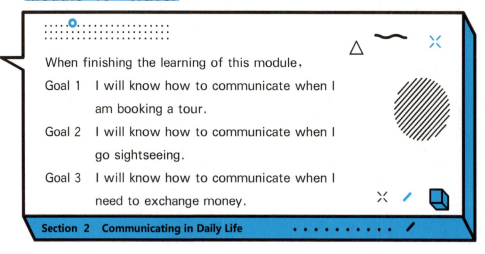

When finishing the learning of this module,

Goal 1 I will know how to communicate when I am booking a tour.

Goal 2 I will know how to communicate when I go sightseeing.

Goal 3 I will know how to communicate when I need to exchange money.

Section 2 Communicating in Daily Life

PRE-TASK

Share one of your most forgettable traveling experiences with your partner.

Your notes

Module 13　Travel

TASK ONE

Booking a Tour

Work in pairs and role-play the conversation.

Agent: Hello Mr Smith, how can I be of assistance today?

Mr. Smith: Good morning. I would like to book a tour for today.

Agent: I can help you with that, what would you like to see?

Mr. Smith: As much of Sydney as possible. What are my choices?

Agent: There are a number of choices to see the sights of Sydney. There's a hop on hop off bus tour that takes you around to the Opera House, The Harbour Bridge and a few other places as well.

Mr. Smith: Do they tell you much about the places on the tour?

Agent: While you're on the bus they give you information about the places you'll visit, but, you explore the locations at your own pace.

Mr. Smith: Is there a set timetable for the tour?

Agent: The buses run in a loop around the city all day. You just get back on when you are ready to go to the next location.

Mr. Smith: What hours do the buses operate?

Agent: They run from 7 a.m. in the morning until 9 p.m. each night.

Mr. Smith: How much do they cost?

Agent: You can buy a pass that lasts all day for $30. You pay when you get on the bus the first time. Here is a map of all the stops.

Mr. Smith: Where's the closest stop?

Agent: Their closest stop is just out at the front of the hotel.

Mr. Smith: That's great. It sounds like a lot of fun. Thanks for your help.

Agent: You're welcome Mr. Smith, enjoy your day.

Work in pairs and orally translate the conversation in your roles in Step 1.

Watch the video "Travel English—Booking a Tour" and note down more expressions for booking a tour. Repeat them after the video.

TASK TWO   Sightseeing

Step 1

There are three conversations about sightseeing. Choose the correct, most natural-sounding responses according to the context of the conversations.

Conversation 1

You: Hello. What time _____ the museum close today?

A. when   B. then   C. does

Museum worker: The museum closes at 7:00 PM.

You: And what time _____ tomorrow?

A. does it open   B. it opens?   C. opening

Museum worker: The museum opens at 9:00 AM.
You: And _____ is the admission?
A. what money　　　　B. what cost　　　　C. how much

Museum worker: The admission fee is $8… $5 if you're a student.
You: And are there any special exhibitions _____ (=happening) right now?
A. off　　　　B. on　　　　C. at

Museum worker: Yes, there's a special exhibition of Edward Hopper's early paintings.
You: Is this _____ in the price of admission?
A. a cost　　　　B. included　　　　C. with

Museum worker: No, there's a separate $5 charge for the exhibition.

Conversation 2
You: Hi, do you have any free _____ of the city
A. carts　　　　B. maps　　　　C. cards

Tourist information center worker: Yes, we do… And we also have a free information booklet.
You: Great. Could we _____ please?
A. have one　　　　B. make it　　　　C. give one

Tourist information center worker: Sure, here you go.
You: We're only here for one day. What _____ that we see?
A. you say　　　　B. do you recommend　　　　C. do you want

Tourist information center worker: Well, you can walk down the Crescent Street. It has some beautiful historic architecture, and some good museums. Actually, that whole neighborhood is very interesting…
You: What's that neighborhood _____?
A. called　　　　B. said　　　　C. known

Tourist information center worker: Uptown. When you go out, just turn right and in about three blocks you'll come to the Crescent Street.

You: Great! We'll _____ it out. Oh, one more thing, could we use your bathroom?

A. look B. take C. check

Tourist information center worker: Of course.

Conversation 3

You: Does the _____ leave from here?

A. sightseeing voyage B. sightseeing journey C. sightseeing tour

Other tourist: Yes, I think so. We're just waiting for the tour guide to arrive.

You: Isn't the tour _____ to start at 4:30?

A. made B. supposed C. have

Other tourist: Yes, it is. I guess the tour guide is running a little late…

(5 minutes later)

Tour guide: I'm sorry everyone, the 4:30 PM tour has been cancelled. We're having some mechanical problems with our bus.

You: So there won't be _____ tours today

A. another B. the C. any more

Tour guide: I'm not sure right now. We'll have to wait and see…

You: How long _____

A. do we have to wait B. to wait C. is the waiting

Tour guide: I'm not sure. They're fixing the bus right now. If they don't fix it in 30 minutes, I'll give all of you your money back.

You: And how long does _____ once it starts

A. the last tour B. the tour last C. the time

Tour guide: About one hour.

Module 13 Travel

Step 2

Work in pairs and role-play the conversations.

TASK THREE
Changing Money

Step 1

Role-play the conversation.

Clerk: What can I do for you?

Traveler: I'd like to change some euros into dollars, please.

Clerk: Certainly. How much would you like to change?

Traveler: Could you tell me what the current exchange rate is?

Clerk: 1.12 U.S. dollars to the euro.

Traveler: And do you charge a commission?

Clerk: No, we don't.

Traveler: In that case, I'll change 500 euros.

Clerk: That makes 560 dollars. Would you prefer your currency in large or small bills?

Traveler: I'd like a mix of both, and could I have some change too?

Clerk: Of course. Please sign here.

BRIDGE TO COLLEGE
交流与表达 2 COMMUNICATION FOR ACADEMIC STUDY (2)

Work in pairs and orally translate the conversation in your roles.

Choose the correct word.

A "bureau de change" is often (1) **located/locating** at a bank, at travel agency, airport, or main railway station-namely, anywhere there is (2) **likely/probable** to be a market for people (3) **needing/need** to convert currency.

Although (4) **origin/originally** French, the term "bureau de change" is widely (5) **using/used** throughout Europe and French-speaking Canada, where it is common to find a sign (6) **says/saying** "exchange" or "change".

In the United States and English-speaking Canada, the business is described (7) **as/like** "currency exchange" or "money exchange", sometimes with various additions such (8) **as/like** "foreign", "desk", "office", "counter", "service", etc.; (9) **for/as example**, "foreign currency exchange office".

When changing money, you should avoid (10) **doing/to do** so at the airport or at your hotel as these tend to offer (11) **worse/worst** exchange rates than elsewhere. It's (12) **usual/usually** cheapest and safest to change money at a bank.

Every (13) **time/times** you buy or sell foreign currency, you have to pay a fee or commission. So if you don't use all your foreign currency, you might want to keep (14) **it/them** until next time you travel. That is unless you know you will not be (15) **travel/travelling** for a while, or it is too much to keep.

Module 13 Travel

ASSIGNMENTS

Role-play in pairs. Suppose one of you is a travel agent, and the other is a tourist to Hangzhou/Xi'an/Suzhou/Tianjin (Select any city you like). Not knowing what tourist attractions (旅游景点) to go, how to get there and where to buy the tickets, the tourist goes to the agent for help. You are required to shot the whole role-playing process and hand in your video work within one week.

BRIDGE TO COLLEGE
交流与表达 2 COMMUNICATION FOR ACADEMIC STUDY (2)

Module 14 Shopping

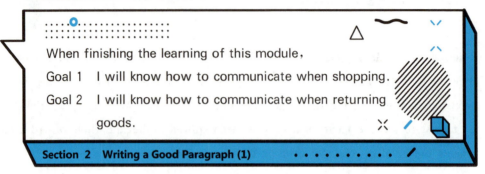

When finishing the learning of this module,
Goal 1   I will know how to communicate when shopping.
Goal 2   I will know how to communicate when returning goods.

Section 2   Writing a Good Paragraph (1)

PRE-TASK

- Watch the videos about four types of stores and note down the important information you think.

- Check your notes in groups of 3 or 4.

Module 14 Shopping

TASK ONE
Learning Communicating When Shopping

Step 1

Listen to an audio and note down how to say as a customer in a department store.

Step 2

Listen to an audio and note down how to say as a customer in a grocery store.

Step 3

Finish the following exercises by choosing the correct, most natural-sounding responses according to the context of the conversations.

Conversation 1

Clerk: Can I help you find something?
You: Yes, do you have this dress in _____?
A. bigger   B. larger   C. a bigger size

BRIDGE TO COLLEGE
交流与表达 2 COMMUNICATION FOR ACADEMIC STUDY (2)

Clerk: What size are you looking for?

You: Size 6... But if you have a size 8, I'll _____ as well.

A. try it on　　　　　　　　B. try to　　　　　　　　C. try for it

Clerk: OK, let me check in the back... (*comes back*) There you go... I found the dress in a size 8...

You: Thanks. Where are your _____ rooms?

A. fitting　　　　　　　　　B. trying　　　　　　　　C. trying-on

Clerk: Just around the corner... Let me know if you need anything else. (*You try on the dress*).

Clerk: So how did that fit?

Clerk: Not too good... I think I need a _____ size.

A. less　　　　　　　　　　B. smaller　　　　　　　　C. not so big

Clerk: That's the smallest size we have in that color... Would you like me to look for another color?

You: No, I like this color... Thanks _____ .

A. anytime　　　　　　　　B. anyway　　　　　　　　C. always

Conversation 2

Store clerk: Can I help you find something?

You: Yes, does this scarf _____ in yellow?

A. arrive　　　　　　　　　B. have　　　　　　　　　C. come

Store clerk: No we don't have it in yellow... only in black, red, and orange.

You: Oh, OK. And it's _____ , right?

A. being sold　　　　　　　B. on sale　　　　　　　　C. on discount

Store clerk: Yes, it is. All our scarves and hats are 20% off today and tomorrow.

You: And _____ the gloves?

A. what　　　　　　　　　B. what if　　　　　　　　C. what about

Module 14　Shopping

Store clerk: They're normal price.
You: These gloves don't have a _____. How much are they?
A. price tag　　　　　　　B. paper　　　　　　　C. information

Store clerk: Those are… $15.99.
You: OK, I'll _____… Could you wrap them up for me? They're a present.
A. take　　　　　　　　B. take them　　　　　　C. purchase

Role-play the conversations in pair.

Step 5

Finish the following exercises by writing the antonyms of each of the highlighted words. Choose from the list below:

big	expensive	loose	dirty	old
long	heavy	hard	cold	dry

1. This cup is _____. Do you have a clean one?
2. This rug looks _____. Do you have a new one?
3. This bicycle is _____. Do you have one that's lighter ?
4. These sleeves are too _____. I prefer short sleeves.
5. This pillow is _____. Do you have a softer one?
6. That car is too _____. I like small cars.
7. These pants are too tight . I usually wear _____ pants.

8. This bowl is wet. Do you have a _____ one?

9. This robe is cheap. The other one was too? _____.

10. This can of Coke is warm. Do you have a _____ one?

TASK TWO

Learning Communicating When You Want to Return Goods

Work in pairs and role-play the conversation.

Assistant: Hi, how can I help you?

Customer: Hi, I'd like to get a refund on this pair of shoes.

Assistant: May I ask why you're returning them?

Customer: I bought them for my son, but they're too big.

Assistant: Did you keep the receipt?

Customer: No, I must have lost it.

Assistant: I'm afraid I can't give you a refund if you don't have the receipt. You can exchange them for a smaller size, or I can give you a credit note.

Customer: OK, I'll take the credit note. How long is it good for?

Assistant: Six months.

Module 14 Shopping

Work in pairs and orally translate the conversation.

Choose the correct word.

If you buy something in a shop and it turns (1) **out/up** to be damaged, broken or faulty in some way, you have a legal right to return the goods and get your money back, as long as they are (2) **always/still** under guarantee.

If you bought something in a shop and then just change your mind (3) **about/ for** it, you do not have any legal right to return the goods. (4) **However/ Therefore**, many shops have a returns policy which lets you (5) **take/to take** your items back to the shop for any reason and get a refund.

Sometimes shops will only let you exchange the goods (6) **by/for** something else in the store, rather than (7) **giving/to give** you a refund. Or they (8) **may/ must** give you a credit note or voucher to use in their store. This is often the case if you're returning something you bought (9) **in/on** a sale.

You'll usually (10) **ought/need** to show where and when you bought your goods. You can (11) **prove/proof** this with your receipt if you have one.

If you don't have a receipt and you bought the items using a debit or credit card, you could ask if they will accept a card statement as the proof of (12) **purchase/ purchasing**.

BRIDGE TO COLLEGE
交流与表达 2 COMMUNICATION FOR ACADEMIC STUDY (2)

Work in pairs and define the words/expressions below.

- faulty
- refund
- voucher
- guarantee
- receipt
- proof
- debit card
- credit note

Check your definitions with another pair by asking and answering questions in turns.

Module 14 Shopping

ASSIGNMENTS

Write the LETTER of the response from the list below to each of the following questions/comments. Choose the best, most logical response.

Part 1

Response	Questions/Comments
1. Do you have a restroom?	a: I'm sorry, we only have that shirt in black.
2. Do you have this in blue?	b: No, but we'll be getting some more tomorrow.
3. I bought this yesterday, but it's too big.	c: I can exchange that for you.
4. Do you have any more of these bags?	d: No, we don't, but we have a mirror.
5. Do you have fitting rooms?	e: No, the one on the right is more expensive.
6. Are these two wallets the same price?	f: Yes, we accept all major credit cards.
7. Can you send these things to my address in Japan?	g: Yes, we accept that currency.
8. Do you accept Master Card?	h: Yes, we can ship your purchased products anywhere in the world.
9. Is there another branch that might have that jacket?	i: Yes, we have another store a couple of blocks away from here.
10. Can I pay with U. S. dollars?	j: Yes, I'll give you a coin, because it's for customers only.

交流与表达 2 COMMUNICATION FOR ACADEMIC STUDY (2)

Part 2

Questions/Comments	Response
1. Can you lower the price a little?	a: 8%
2. Are all of these on sale?	b: Yes, I can put it on hold for two hours.
3. Do I have to buy a converter for this computer?	c: No, but there's a convenience store that sells groceries.
4. How much is the tax here?	d: About two hours.
5. Do you sell souvenirs?	e: Yes, we have refrigerator magnets and coffee cups.
6. How much is this?	f: OK, but only by a couple of dollars.
7. How much time will it take to make this?	g: Yes, I put it in your bag.
8. Can you set this aside for me?	h: No, it comes with a universal power source.
9. Did you give me my receipt?	i: Each item has a price tag underneath.
10. Is there a supermarket around here?	j: Yes, all the ties are on sale.

Module 15　Visiting a Doctor

Module 15　Visiting a Doctor

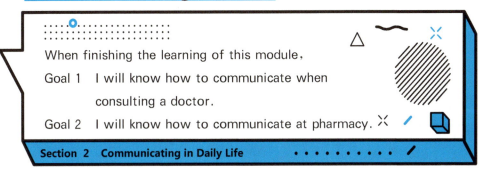

When finishing the learning of this module,
Goal 1　I will know how to communicate when consulting a doctor.
Goal 2　I will know how to communicate at pharmacy.
Section 2　Communicating in Daily Life

PRE-TASK

- Please translate the following nouns into English.

牙医	儿科医生	内科医生
外科医生	妇科医生	眼科医生
门诊（部）	急诊	住院部
病房	症状	胶囊
口服液	片剂	丸剂

- Watch a video "Seeing a Doctor" and read after it. Note down the terms or expressions if necessary.

TASK ONE

Learning Background

Choose the correct word.

If you are feeling ill or **(1)have/having** a medical problem, you can **(2)make/do** an appointment to see the doctor. In Britain, the place where doctors see their patients is **(3)calling/called** a surgery. In America, it's a doctor's office.

When you arrive for your **(4) appointment/meeting**, the secretary or receptionist will probably **(5)ask/say** you to wait in the waiting room until the doctor is ready to see you.

When you finally get to see the doctor, he **(6)is/will** usually begin by asking you to describe your **(7)symptom/symptoms**. He may then give you an **(8)exam/examination**, and take your blood pressure, for example.

If the doctor knows what's **(9)wrong/matter** with you, he will give you some **(10)advice/advices** and perhaps prescribe **(11)some/the** medicine. You will have to take the prescription to the chemist's to get the medicine.

(12)Hopefully/Luckily, you will get well soon!

Work in groups of 3 or 4 and have a discussion about the following questions.

Try use the communication skills you've learned in Module 9 if you cannot find the exact words to express yourself.

Module 15   Visiting a Doctor

1. How often do you go to the doctor's?
2. When and why did you last go to see the doctor?
3. How are you feeling at the moment?
4. What's the health service like in your country?
5. Would you like to be a doctor?

TASK TWO
Learning to Communicate When Seeing a Doctor

Step 1

Role-play the following conversation.

Doctor: Good morning, Mrs Jones. What seems to be the problem?

Patient: Well doctor, I've got a sore throat and a bad cough. I've also got a headache.

Doctor: How long have you had these symptoms?

Patient: About four days now, and I'm feeling really tired too.

Doctor: It sounds like you've got the flu. Take two aspirin every four hours. You should also get lots of rest and drink plenty of fluids. And if you don't feel better in a couple of days, give me a call.

Patient: Thank you doctor.

BRIDGE TO COLLEGE
交流与表达 2 COMMUNICATION FOR ACADEMIC STUDY (2)

Underline the formulaic expressions of the doctor in the conversation above.

Watch the video "Health Problems" to learn how to express the symptoms. Note down the terms and repeat them after the video.

Your note

Module 15　Visiting a Doctor

TASK THREE
Learning Where and How to Buy Medecine

Watch the video "How to Buy Medicine in English" and note down the important information related to where and how to buy medicine.

Your note

Check your notes with a partner.

BRIDGE TO COLLEGE
交流与表达 2　COMMUNICATION FOR ACADEMIC STUDY (2)

ASSIGNMENTS

1. Watch the video "Health Problems" to learn more about how to express the symptoms. Read after the video. Note down the terms and repeat them after the video.

2. Watch two more videos and learn more expressions.
   - Video 1　Medical Vocabulary

   - Video 2　Part of the Body

Module 16　Asking and Giving Directions

Module 16　Asking and Giving Directions

When finishing the learning of this module,

Goal 1　I will know how to ask directions in English.

Goal 2　I will know how to give directions in English.

Section 2　Communicating in Daily Life

PRE-TASK

- Please write down three sentences about asking directions and three equivalent answers for giving directions.

    - _____
    - _____
    - _____

- Work in groups of 3 or 4 and have a discussion about the following questions.
    - If you encounter someone who wants to ask for directions, can you give your instructions clearly?
    - If you can't, what is the problem?
    - If you can, what are the possible methods to clearly show the way?

BRIDGE TO COLLEGE
交流与表达 ❷ COMMUNICATION FOR ACADEMIC STUDY (2)

##
Learning to Ask for Directions

Watch a video "English at University (2)—Learn phrases about asking for directions" and note down the expressions about asking for directions.

Your notes

Work individually. According to the video, summarize the possible tips of asking for directions in English from other English Learners.

Module 16　Asking and Giving Directions

Work in groups of 3 or 4 and share your summary.

Tips of asking for directions

TASK TWO

Giving Directions

Read the information box as followed.

Etiquette of Giving Directions

1. This is not a time for small talk. Use basic English to offer directions. Short phrases are best.
2. Do the best you can. Speak slowly and use very careful pronunciation. Spell out a word if necessary.

BRIDGE TO COLLEGE
交流与表达 2 COMMUNICATION FOR ACADEMIC STUDY (2)

Expressions for Giving directions

■ The easiest way is to…

■ The quickest way is to…

■ The best way is to…

◆ go + direction (right, left, down, up, through)

◆ take + road name

◆ turn + right/left

◆ stay on + road name for + distance or time

● Use transitions: Separate each leg of the route with a transition.

after that

then

next

when you get to… go…

finally

Step 2

Watch the first part of the video "How to Ask for Directions and How to Give Directions" and note down the information related to giving directions.

Your notes

Module 16 Asking and Giving Directions

Step 3

Work individually and figure out some tips for giving clear directions according to the video.

> **Note down the tips**

Step 4

Work in groups of 3 or 4 and share your tips.

BRIDGE TO COLLEGE
交流与表达 2 COMMUNICATION FOR ACADEMIC STUDY (2)

TASK THREE
Practicing Asking for and Giving Directions

Watch the first part of the video "Not Afraid to Ask for Directions—Brain Games", and work out the route on the map given according to what you hear in the video.

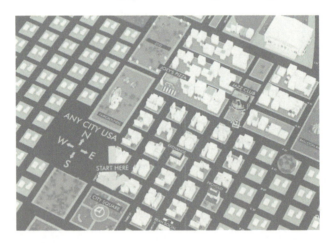

Watch the whole video and answer the question below.

- What does "Brain Games" mean in this video?

SECTION 3

Making One-Minute Presentations

Module 17   Making a Good One-Minute Presentation

Module 17   Making a Good One-Minute Presentation

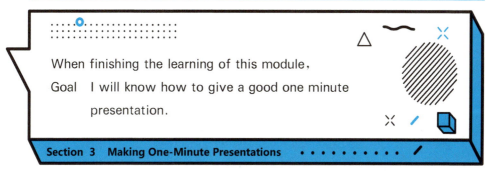

Goal When finishing the learning of this module, I will know how to give a good one minute presentation.

Section 3   Making One-Minute Presentations

TASK ONE
Understanding a Presetation

Read the notes card below and learn the strategies.

What is a Presentation?

A presentation is a means of communication that can be adapted to various speaking situations, such as talking to a group, addressing a meeting or briefing a team.

A presentation can also be used as a broad term that encompasses other "speaking engagements" such as making a speech at a wedding or getting a point across in a video conference.

To be effective, step-by-step preparation and the method and means of presenting the information should be carefully considered.

BRIDGE TO COLLEGE
交流与表达 2 COMMUNICATION FOR ACADEMIC STUDY (2)

Step 2

Work in group with the questions below and have a discussion on "*How to make a good one-minute presentation?*" with the questions below. Note down the results of your discussion and get prepared for a presentation to show the results in one minute.

Questions:

1. In what way can we start a one-minute presentation?
2. Can we use a story or joke to attract our audiences attention? Why or why not?
3. With the same topic, what difference(s) are there in one-minute presentation and three-minute presentation?

Results of your discussion

Module 17　Making a Good One-Minute Presentation

TASK TWO
Giving a One-Minute Presentation

Giving a one-minute presentation

Write down the questions you need to ask to determine the information in the Survey Chart on the next page.

1. _____
2. _____
3. _____
4. _____
5. _____
6. _____
7. _____
8. _____
9. _____
10. _____

BRIDGE TO COLLEGE
交流与表达 2 COMMUNICATION FOR ACADEMIC STUDY (2)

Survey Chart

1. Family name: _____   Given name: _____

2. Place of birth: _____

3. Education: _____

4. Started learning English in: _____

5. Reason for learning English: _____

6. Interests/Hobbies: _____

7. Skills: _____

8. Good/bad qualities: _____

9. Ambitions: _____

10. Other information: _____

Step 2

Now use the questions to interview a partner. Write down his or her answers in the Survey Chart.

Module 17　Making a Good One-Minute Presentation

Get prepared for a one-minute presentation to introduce the partner you interviewed in Step 2.

ASSIGNMENTS

Get ready for a one-minute presentation to tell an *unforgettable* story happened in your childhood.

Friendly reminders

- How do you start a story? Go to the story directly or⋯?
- How do you use speed and pauses in telling a story?

Module 18 Expanding Ideas in Presentation: Description

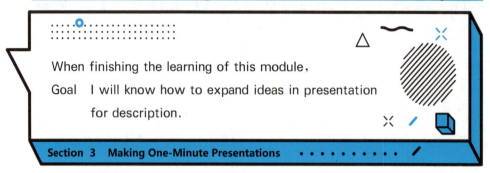

Goal: When finishing the learning of this module, I will know how to expand ideas in presentation for description.

Section 3 Making One-Minute Presentations

TASK ONE
Recognizing Descriptive Words and Expressions

Read the following note card and underline the important information.

Descriptive words are basically key Words and Phrases that help paint a clear picture and tell a story about something, whether you are writing an article, describing a project or promoting a product. Descriptive words are important as they give clear messages to the readers and listeners.

Module 18 Expanding Ideas in Presentation: Description

Examples

- **Descriptive words for personal traits and characteristics**

  active   courageous   self-reliant   sincere   dependable   alert

  broad-minded   challenge-oriented   risk-taker   far-sighted

  enthusiastic   attentive   trustworthy   competent

- **Descriptive words for touch and feel**

  fragile   moist   oily   slippery   furry   crisp   rough

  wet   wooly   sticky   leathery   silky   tepid   elastic

  hairy   slimy   textured   damp   gritty   spongy

  rubbery   sandy

- **Descriptive words for positive emotions**

  alive   delighted   thrilled   joyful   ecstatic   amused

  cheerful   content   merry   jovial   elated   pleased

  ...

Work in groups and make a list of words and expressions to describe a person.

Your word bank

BRIDGE TO COLLEGE
交流与表达 ❷ COMMUNICATION FOR ACADEMIC STUDY (2)

TASK TWO
Organizing the Ideas in Presentation for Description

 **ACTIVITY 1** ▶

Understanding presentations for description

Read the following note card and underline the important information

A descriptive rhetorical style is one that uses the five sense (touch, taste, sight, sound, smell) and other details to provide the reader/listener with a vivid idea or picture of what is being represented.

http://owl.excelsior.edu/rhetorical—styles/descriptive—essay

Guidelines for preparing a description

- **Take time to brainstorm**

  Make sure that you jot down some ideas before you begin describing it. For instance, if you choose pizza, you might start by writing down a few words: sauce, cheese, crust, pepperoni, sausage, spices, hot, melted, etc. Once you have written down some words, you can begin by compiling descriptive lists for each one.

- **Use clear and concise language**

  This means that words are chosen carefully, particularly for their relevancy in relation to that which you are intending to describe.

Module 18 Expanding Ideas in Presentation: Description

- **Use senses**

    Remember, if you are describing something, you need to be appealing to the senses of the reader/listener. Explain how the thing smelled, felt, sounded, tasted, or looked. Embellish the moment with senses.

- **Be organized**

    Strive to present an organized and logical description.

Work in groups and have a discussion on "*What is important for describing X in one minute?*".

Results of your discussion

Giving a one-minute presentation

Secretly choose one classmate to describe (appearance, characteristics and personal traits). The following expressions may be helpful for your description.

BRIDGE TO COLLEGE
交流与表达 2 COMMUNICATION FOR ACADEMIC STUDY (2)

- adventurous: likes to try new or exciting things
- energetic: has a lot of energy and is very active
- clumsy: always accidentally breaking or hitting things
- fair: treats everyone equally and in a reasonable way
- ambitious: determined to be successful, rich or famous
- concerned: worried about something
- industrious: always working very hard
- sympathetic: easily understands the feelings of other people
- bossy: likes to tell other people what to do
- decisive: makes choices or decides what to do quickly and confidently.
- easygoing: relaxed, calm, and easy to get along with
- curious: always wants to find out about something
- graceful: shows good manners and respect for other people
- bold: confident and not afraid of people
- cautious: careful to avoid problems or danger

Step 2

Present your descriptions in one minute to the class. Let them try to guess who is being described.

ASSIGNMENTS

Get prepared for a one-minute presentation to describe one of the four seasons in your hometown. When describing, please use descriptive words of senses to image a vivid picture to the audience.

BRIDGE TO COLLEGE
交流与表达 2 COMMUNICATION FOR ACADEMIC STUDY (2)

Module 19 Expanding Ideas in Presentation: Giving Definition

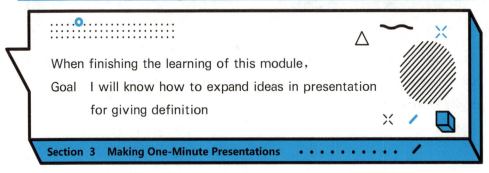

Goal   When finishing the learning of this module, I will know how to expand ideas in presentation for giving definition

Section 3   Making One-Minute Presentations

TASK ONE
Recognizing How to Develop a Definition

Watch the video "*What is groundwater?*", and note down the important information.

Your notes

Module 19 Expanding Ideas in Presentation: Giving Definition

Watch the video again and have a group discussion on the question: "*How does the speaker explain the term groundwater?*". Note down the results of your discussion.

Results of your discussion

According to what you have got from Step 1 and Step 2, summarize how to develop a definition.

Your summary

TASK TWO
Organizing the Ideas in Presentation for Giving Definition

Step 1

Watch the video "What is artificial intelligence?", and note down the important information.

Your notes

Step 2

Share your notes with the partner. Make sure all the important information is included.

Step 3

Prepare a one-minute presentation on "What is artificial intelligence?" with the help of your notes.

Module 19 Expanding Ideas in Presentation: Giving Definition

Work in pairs and share the presentation with your partner.

ASSIGNMENTS

Get prepared for a one-minute presentation to define _____.

BRIDGE TO COLLEGE
交流与表达 ❷ COMMUNICATION FOR ACADEMIC STUDY (2)

Module 20 Expanding Ideas in Presentation: Classification

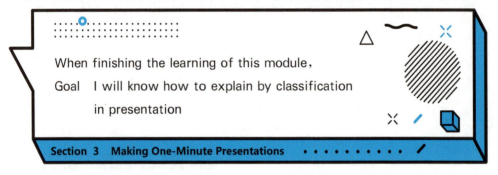

Goal When finishing the learning of this module, I will know how to explain by classification in presentation

Section 3   Making One-Minute Presentations

TASK ONE
Recognizing How to Make Classification

Watch the video "*Talking about future*" and note down the important information.

Your notes

Module 20 Expanding Ideas in Presentation: Classification

Step 2

Watch the video again and have a group discussion on the question: *"How does the speaker explain how to talk about the future?"*. Note down the result of your discussion.

Results of your discussion

Step 3

According to what you have got from Step 1 and Step 2, summarize how to explain by classification.

Your summary

TASK TWO
Organizing the Ideas in Presentation by Classification

Watch the video in TASK ONE again and get more familiar with the details.

Your notes

Share your notes with the partner. Make sure all the important information is included in your notes.

Module 20 Expanding Ideas in Presentation: Classification

Make a one-minute presentation on "Talking about the future" with the help of your notes. Classification is needed when organizing the ideas in your speech.

ASSIGNMENTS

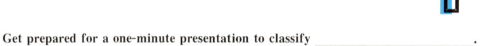

Get prepared for a one-minute presentation to classify _____.

BRIDGE TO COLLEGE
交流与表达 ❷ COMMUNICATION FOR ACADEMIC STUDY (2)

Module 21　Expanding Ideas in Presentation: Process

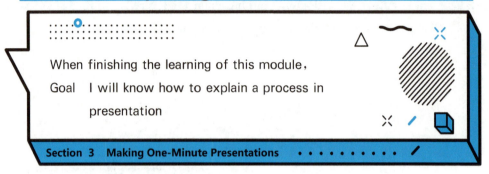

Goal　When finishing the learning of this module, I will know how to explain a process in presentation

Section 3　Making One-Minute Presentations

TASK ONE
Recognizing How to Explain a Process

Step 1

Watch the video "*How to review workout history in the Activity app*" and note down the important information.

Your notes

Module 21 Expanding Ideas in Presentation: Process

Step 2

Watch the video again and have a group discussion on the question: "*How does the speaker explain how to review workout history in the Activity app?*". Note down the result of your discussion.

Results of your discussion

Step 3

According to what you have got from Step 1 and Step 2, summarize how to explain a process.

Your summary

TASK TWO
Organizing the Ideas in Presentation by Process

Step 1

Brainstorm the suitable topics for explaining a process.

Your notes

Step 2

Share your topics with the partner. Choose one topic, and list all the steps in the process.

Steps in the process
1.
2.
3.
...

Module 21 Expanding Ideas in Presentation: Process

Step 3

Make a one-minute presentation on "How to …" with the help of your list. Pay attention to the transitions between different steps.

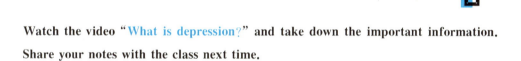
ASSIGNMENTS

Watch the video "What is depression?" and take down the important information. Share your notes with the class next time.

BRIDGE TO COLLEGE
交流与表达 2 COMMUNICATION FOR ACADEMIC STUDY (2)

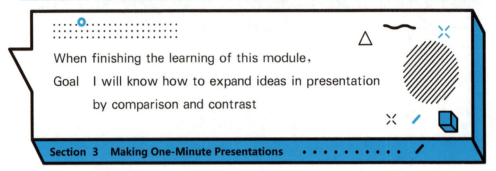

Module 22 Expanding Ideas in Presentation: Comparison and Contrast

Goal   When finishing the learning of this module, I will know how to expand ideas in presentation by comparison and contrast

Section 3   Making One-Minute Presentations

TASK ONE
Recognizing How to Make Comparison and Contrast

Step 1

Watch the video "What is depression?", which was your assignment in Module 21. Check your notes related to the differences between feeling depressed and having depression.

Your notes

Module 22 Expanding Ideas in Presentation: Comparison and Contrast

Step 2

Share your notes with your group member and have a discussion on the question: "*How does the speaker explain the differences between feeling depressed and having depression?*". Note down the results of your discussion.

Results of your discussion

Step 3

According to what you have got from Step 1 and Step 2, summarize how to express comparison and contrast.

Your summary

TASK TWO
Organizing the Ideas in Presentation by Comparison and Contrast

Brainstorm the suitable topics for comparison and contrast.

Your notes

Share your topics with the partner. Choose one topic, and list all the aspects to be compared.

_____ (your topic)

Aspects to be compared

1.
2.
3.
...

Module 22 Expanding Ideas in Presentation: Comparison and Contrast

Make a one-minute presentation on "... *vs.* ..." with the help of your list. Pay attention to the transitions between different aspects.

ASSIGNMENTS

Build your word bank for comparison and contrast.

COMPARISON	CONTRAST

Module 23 Expanding Ideas in Presentation: Cause and Effect

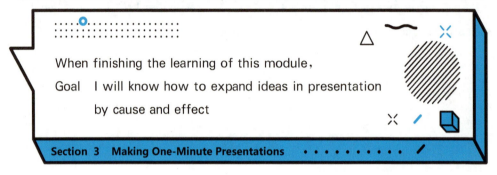

Goal When finishing the learning of this module, I will know how to expand ideas in presentation by cause and effect

Section 3 Making One-Minute Presentations

TASK ONE
Recognizing the Relation Between Cause and Effect

Step 1

Watch the video "Stress and Our Body", and note down the important information.

Your notes

Module 23　Expanding Ideas in Presentation: Cause and Effect

Step 2

Share your notes with your group member and have a discussion on the question: "*How does the speaker explain what stress will bring to our body?*". Note down the result of your discussion.

Results of your discussion

Step 3

According to what you have got from Step 1 and Step 2, summarize how to explain the relation between cause and effect.

Your summary

BRIDGE TO COLLEGE
交流与表达 2 COMMUNICATION FOR ACADEMIC STUDY (2)

TASK TWO
Organizing the Ideas in Presentation by Cause and Effect

Step 1

Brainstorm the suitable topics for explaining cause and effect.

Your notes

Step 2

Share your topics with the partner. Choose one topic, and list all the aspects to be explained.

	Cause	Effect
1.		
2.		
3.		
...		

Module 23 Expanding Ideas in Presentation: Cause and Effect

Step 3

Make a one-minute presentation with the help of your list. Pay attention to the expressions for showing cause and effect.

ASSIGNMENTS

Build your word bank for cause and effect.

CAUSE	EFFECT

BRIDGE TO COLLEGE
交流与表达 ❷ COMMUNICATION FOR ACADEMIC STUDY (2)

Module 24 Expanding Ideas in Presentation: Problem–Solution

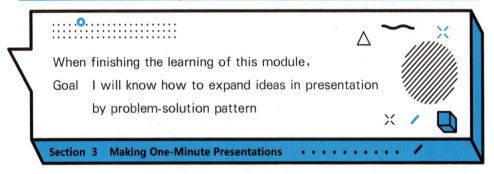

Goal: When finishing the learning of this module, I will know how to expand ideas in presentation by problem-solution pattern

Section 3 Making One-Minute Presentations

TASK ONE
Recognizing Problem-Solution Pattern

Watch the video "*How to take notes faster*", and note down the important information.

Your notes

Module 24 Expanding Ideas in Presentation: Problem-Solution

Step 2

Share your notes with your group member, and have a discussion on the questions list below:

1. What is the problem mentioned in the video?
2. How does the speaker explain the ways to solve the problem?

Note down the results of your discussion.

> **Results of your discussion**
>
>

Step 3

According to what you have got from Step 1 and Step 2, summarize how to explain by problem-solution pattern.

> **Your summary**
>
>

TASK TWO
Organizing the Ideas in Presentation by Problem-Solution

Brainstorm the problems in your daily life.

Your notes

Share your problems with the partner. Choose one, and list all the ways or methods to solve the problem.

Problem

Solutions

Module 24 Expanding Ideas in Presentation: Problem−Solution

Make a one-minute presentation with the help of your list. Pay attention to the expressions for showing problem-solution.

ASSIGNMENTS

Get prepared for a one-minute presentation on "How to release your stress?"

BRIDGE TO COLLEGE
交流与表达 2 COMMUNICATION FOR ACADEMIC STUDY (2)

Module 25 Expanding Ideas in Presentation: Argumentation

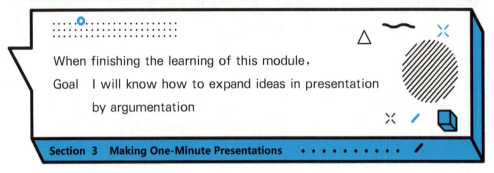

Goal When finishing the learning of this module, I will know how to expand ideas in presentation by argumentation

Section 3 Making One-Minute Presentations

TASK ONE
Recognizing Argumentation

Watch the video "History vs. Christopher Columbus", and note down the important information.

Your notes

Module 25 Expanding Ideas in Presentation: Argumentation

Step 2

Share your notes with your group member and have a discussion (according to what you've got from the video) on the question: "Was Columbus an intrepid explorer or a ruthless exploiter?". Note down the results of your discussion.

Results of your discussion

Step 3

According to what you have got from Step 1 and Step 2, summarize what the term "argue" means and how to argue in a logical way.

Your summary

BRIDGE TO COLLEGE
交流与表达 ❷ COMMUNICATION FOR ACADEMIC STUDY (2)

TASK TWO
Organizing the Ideas in Presentation by Argumentation

Step 1

Brainstorm the suitable topics for showing your opinions.

> **Your notes**

Step 2

Share your topics with the partner. Choose one, and list at least three supporting points. Think about the evidence of each supporting idea.

> **Your argument point of view**
>
> Supporting point 1
>
> Supporting point 2
>
> Supporting point 3

Module 25 Expanding Ideas in Presentation: Argumentation

Make a one-minute presentation with the help of your list. (There is no need to mention all the supporting points in your list, due to the time limitation.)

- Pay attention to the expressions for showing one's opinions.

ASSIGNMENTS

Build your expression bank for arguing "for…" and arguing "against…".

FOR	AGAINST